THE TOWER *of* BABBLE

THE
TOWER *of*
BABBLE

Michael Parish

ALTO ZEPHYR
Oakland, California

Alto Zephyr
2115 Central Avenue, Suite 1
Alameda, California 94501

Printed in the United States of America on acid-free paper.

Library of Congress Control Number: 2020905765
ISBN 978-0-578-65952-7 (paperback)
ISBN 978-0-578-66824-6 (epub)

FIRST, to my unbelievably wonderful
family, Maya, Billy, Mark, Wahleah, Tohaana,
Alowaan, Zephyr (now six months old),
the James Gang, and of course Mary-Jo—
who read every word and supplied most of
the commas to brake my breakneck style.
And to Susan, without whom there wouldn't
be such a wonderful family to begin with.
Bless you all. You are my blessing to be sure.

THEN to the Princeton Class of '65—
whose secretary I have been for more than
thirty years, and who have given me great joy
and helped me hone my writing abilities, to
whatever extent you discern them to be honed.

AND FINALLY, to my most constant
and closest readers/editors, unpaid but
diligent and thorough—Tony Nuland, Dan
Kleinman, Max Morrow, and Don Irwin—
The Four Horsemen of the Apostrophe!!

CONTENTS

FINAL INTRODUCTION*

Without question, the greatest invention in the history of humankind is the zero. Without nothing, there cannot truly be something, because everything needs its opposite to become complete. Two brief examples will suffice.

My dear friend and former law partner Richard Cole was handed the chairmanship of our Wall Street firm's Associates' Lunch, a once-a-month gathering of all lawyers, not just associates. It was always well attended, at a fancy business club nearby. The partners ate thousands of meals there every year, excellent meals, which were deducted for tax purposes because they were business-related. The chairmanship was a nothing job, and Richard did it to perfection. On one unusual occasion, the senior partner attended, and while Richard was making his introductory remarks, that man happened to knock over his water glass. Without missing a beat, Richard spread his hands wide and announced that everyone should now knock over their own water glass, but it was not mandatory—in other words, an order that need not be obeyed. He got the laugh he deserved, no more water was spilled, but that remark completed the event and allowed us to move on. Perfect in every way.

The other example was the greatest trade in NBA history, that of Dick Van Arsdale for his identical twin, Tom. The twins

---

* I call this the final introduction for the paradox involved in the phrase and because the first version was no good, but this one is. Take my word for it, since it's the only one you will see.

switched uniforms between Indianapolis and Phoenix, but otherwise nothing changed. They had played together, both All-Americans, at Indiana University, but it was clear to the league on draft date that they should not be allowed to play for the same team, because that would be too good and possibly lead to cries of conspiracy. So they went their separate ways. During their careers before the trade, they each played point guard, and their statistics, in points per game, free throw percentages, assists, time lost to injuries, fouls, and probably in the total amount of soap they used while showering both after games and throughout their lives, were identical, to a tenth of a percentage point—or cake of soap, as the case may be.

So one year, as the trading deadline approached, the general managers of those two teams came up with the astonishingly brilliant stroke of swapping their star point guards. After the trade, the Arsdales' performances continued to be essentially mirror images of each other. But, just as on Wall Street when we use the term "Activity as the proxy for progress," the general managers did something, which they definitely could not fail to do, but also did nothing, because that was all they could reasonably do in the circumstances.

On the flight back to California after my fiftieth law school reunion, it came to me that I had been retired for fifteen years. Not having been in legal practice for that extended period, I told myself that if I limited my scope to true stories, there was a chance that people would actually believe me. That's what this book is. Forty-three true stories about my life and also about some other occurrences that I know absolutely to be true. I believe there is not nearly enough laughter and humor in our world now, or in the world altogether since the dawn of time, so I want to do my part to change that as much as one man can, which is as close to nothing as there is, but also not nothing at all.

Enjoy every word! I know I have. Best wishes to all.

Michael Parish
2020

THE TOWER *of* BABBLE

I

NINETY-NINE PERCENT OF LAWYERS GIVE THE REST OF US A BAD NAME

DUE TO PRACTICING LAW with a large New York City firm for thirty years as a partner doing corporate finance, I was fortunate to be served for many of my financial needs by the private banking group of a large bank with a household name; I even had an individual assigned to me. After a few years of perfectly happy interactions with a series of such individuals, I was lucky enough to be assisted by a genuine jewel of a woman who often anticipated my needs and, if not, always took care of business promptly and skillfully. This included covering otherwise bounceable checks, acquiring co-op apartments and financing the same, and finally obtaining a home equity line of credit (HELOC), since cash flow—when you were rising in the firm and annually needed both to live on what you expected to earn and to keep repatriating part of the money into the firm—was a balancing act year in and year out.

After the HELOC was in place, I called Marion to thank her both for this latest matter and for the whole succession of well-performed exercises. She kindly expressed her appreciation for my business and for being so easy to work with, and on the spur of the moment I asked, having never met her face to face, if I could buy her lunch as a way to express my thanks. She made a small giggle and then said she would love that, and we set a date and a place, a northern Italian restaurant a block from my office, with linen tablecloths and good food, although when you got the check you saw that you were also funding the midtown location, the décor, and the starch in the waiters' always speck-less jackets.

She was already seated when I arrived and waved away my apologies for being five minutes late. I knew from prior con-versations that she had high-school-aged twins from her now-ended marriage and a steady boyfriend with whom she enjoyed taking motorcycle trips with his club on weekends, so I was a little surprised, but pleasantly so, at how elegantly turned out she was—again reflecting, while mocking my addiction to this habit of observation by one who had grown up in very modest circumstances, that I must have at least paid for the tasteful low heels I noticed when she stood up to greet me.

We toasted the occasion with a simple glass of white wine, had a little bit of small talk about our families and vacation plans, and gave our orders to the waiter. Then she put her glass down and said, "This is really a very nice place, and there's something I want to share with you." Little as I knew her, I had completely no idea what that might be, but, as Ross Perot said in a debate the year he helped Bill Clinton into the White House, I was "all ears" and just inquired what that might be.

"Well," she said, "I've been working in our private banking group for almost eighteen years now, you know, and it's a good job, since I do deal mostly with people who are smart and edu-cated and successful and have excellent manners." She stopped for a moment, and I nodded in encouragement for her to go on.

"And here's the thing," she continued. "In all that time with all those people, you're the first one who ever bought me lunch, or even a drink." We both sputtered with laughter and, that topic having been fully addressed, changed the subject, although I have often remembered the story during my further dealings with our profession.

II WHAT MAKES SOMEONE "A GOOD LAWYER"?

THE HEAD OF THE FIRM where I worked for more than twenty years liked to tell the story of how a friend had helped him define the meaning of "a good lawyer." The friend received an appointment as an assistant U.S. Attorney for the Southern District of New York, something nobody would sneeze at, since it's the most prominent and prestigious U.S. Attorney's Office in the country. The *New York Law Journal*, a semiofficial publication widely read in the legal community both for news and for information regarding cases, schedules, and other official legal business, would publish a small notice on its front page concerning every such appointment, so his name and particulars appeared there in that fashion.

On his second day, he received a call from a woman speaking in a low voice and saying—this was previous to our current elongated state of derangement about national security—that she had information about an important matter concerning a subject which she could not talk about over the telephone, but was sure he would want to know about and would hopefully address. She asked if he might be available in an hour or so, since she lived downtown close to his offices. His calendar not having started to get crowded, he consented.

She arrived on schedule, and he showed her into his sparsely decorated new office, observing that she appeared to be of late middle age and was plainly and neatly dressed, and that she carried only her purse, rather than any folders or document case. She quickly explained, leaning forward and dropping her voice, that she was being spied upon by Martians, who could witness everything she did and also see through her clothes, which was agonizing, and she hadn't been able to stop them or get them to leave. He asked if she had contacted anyone else and she responded affirmatively, citing other assistant U.S. Attorneys in his office. "But they always say they can't help or call back later and tell me the same thing. You know, I'm sure these Martians are everywhere, but the people they spy on are too fearful or just don't know what to do. But you can bet your life that I'm not the only one that's suffering through this horrible situation—that's why I need to keep making the effort, because it's really a nation-wide problem, if people really knew what's going on!"

He put his fingers together in front of him, tip to tip, and reflected on what she had said. In front of him the desk was empty except for a telephone, in and out boxes, and a desk pad with the standard green blotter in it and a small pile of yellow legal pads. Alongside that were two pencil cups, filled with sharpened pencils, a stapler with boxes of extra staples, a tape dispenser, scissors, and a box of paper clips. He reached for the box of clips and stood up to hand it to her. Remaining standing, he asked her to open it and put two of the paper clips together, which she did.

"Now, you know how to make a chain out of these, don't you?" he asked in a friendly, matter-of-fact way, and she nodded. He sat back down and continued, "Now, if you make a chain out of these that goes all the way around your waist, and then add another chain on the side that goes down your side to just above your hemline, which you can do in our ladies' room before you leave the building, that will render you invisible to these Martians and they will stop bothering you, because they won't know how to find you and they will get frustrated and go away. But you need to not tell anyone about this, over the phone or in person, because that will alert them and they will take countermeasures to defeat our plan. Do you understand me? Do you have any questions? Stop in the ladies' room, do as I've outlined, and—abracadabra!—you'll have your life back and not be troubled anymore."

She popped out of her chair and came around the desk to give him a hug of thanks, which he managed to forestall somewhat by taking hold of the shoulder of her leading arm and putting his other arm on her other shoulder. With that, he helped her back around to pick up her purse, walked her to the door, saw her out with a pat on the back, and she was never seen or heard from again.

"Now that's a good lawyer," my senior partner would say. "Takes the time to analyze the problem, considers his resources, his or hers, fits the solution to the client's particular needs and circumstances, makes sure the client is satisfied and has no further questions, and sticks the landing. Who could want more? He, or she, also recognizes, courtesy of the great legal text *Animal Farm*, that, just as all animals are equal, but some are more equal than others. All clients are crazy—because by definition they are crazy or they would never have to resort to our profession—but some are a little crazier than others."

III SOMETIMES YOU FEEL LIKE A NUT, SOMETIMES YOU DON'T

WHEN I HEAR THAT JINGLE, I think of the episode of *Candid Camera* where they told a young man that the room he was in had various beams of invisible light crossing it, said generally where they were, and told him he'd win a nice, specified, cash prize if he could move around the room and pick up five objects without encountering any of the beams. He went about it slowly and meticulously, pausing regularly, and at one point he sang that jingle to himself to calm his nerves. Then sang it again.

Last week at our local senior center I attended a nutrition lecture that featured nuts as one of the topics, so I thought of that man but decided to go anyway. The speaker started out by observing how many nuts are among the most nutritious foods available to us, pausing to note that it was important not to salt them too much or add too much oil to them, for fairly obvious reasons.

This comment took me back to freshman year in college when my roommate, during our first week together, asked if I wanted to see what he learned in prep school and, without waiting for a reply, produced a nickel pack of Planters Peanuts (now a fifty-cent bag) and one of those glass ashtrays that was an inverted pyramid with the top cut off and places for a cigarette on each corner. He poured the nuts into the center of the bowl and lit a match, then set it next to one edge of the pile. In fifteen seconds, the flame from the nuts was about eighteen inches high, and in another fifteen seconds, the ashtray burst into a hundred pieces from the heat. So I knew the speaker was on the money with that.

6

She next referred to the plastic jars of mixed nuts, about a quart size, sold at Costco, Trader Joe's, Safeway, and many such stores. These are pretty standardized, she said, and all of them contain six varieties of real nuts, so peanuts are not included because they are legumes. The six varieties are cashews, almonds, pecans, walnuts, Brazil nuts, and macadamia nuts.

She then asked us to guess which of these is the most nourishing and which the least popular, according to scientific data and consumer polls, respectively. Many people chose cashews or macadamias as the most nutritious, leading her to ask if they also believed in Santa Claus, the Easter Bunny, and the Tooth Fairy, which got a laugh from the rest of us. She then tempered her remark by adding that these people could be seen as wishful thinkers, but also as optimists. The answer, she said, was Brazil nuts, partly because they contain selenium, which none of the others do in nearly the same amount, if at all.

I had always thought Brazil nuts were in the jar because they were so large, and thus took up a lot of space, and must be cheaper than the other nuts to grow and process. I continue to doubt that they are in there for their nutritious qualities, but I am neither a wishful thinker (I think) nor much of an optimist, at my age and in our current age.

As to the least popular, most people did guess Brazil nuts, with about a quarter opting for walnuts because of their bitterness. She agreed with our majority and said there was a basic lesson here—the thing you like the least is almost always best for you. Life in a nutshell, as it were.

IV THE BROWN DERBY

THAT WAS AL SMITH'S SOBRIQUET when he was governor of New York and a presidential candidate against Hoover in 1928. It served to emphasize, like his accent, his connection to real people, and not to the "swells" who have always been at the center of politics and power in our country. A favorite pub of mine in New York has a framed photo of Babe Ruth wearing a "Smith for President" button, with a half-smoked cigar in the corner of his mouth and a derby on his head. During the time Smith was governor, the father of a friend of mine, a lawyer, lived on the Lower East Side, was Jewish, and was interested in politics, especially since a number of Jews had replaced earlier residents, but the area was dominated by Italians, who were largely Democrats.

He was a protégé of the Republican leader, "Boss" Koenig, famous for the truism "You can't beat someone with no one," who offered to support my friend's father in what looked like a hopeless race, just to have a candidate. At one point early in the campaign, he had a sit-down with his opponent, that man's bodyguards, and his own, having stipulated in advance that everyone would put their firearms on the table at the beginning. He ran against very long odds but won by six votes, his first victory in a long line leading to a substantial career in statewide office. The Assembly was then composed of people with single-year terms. When he arrived in Albany and was sworn in at the Statehouse, he immediately received a message from the governor saying his presence was required "on the Second Floor," as the governor's office is still commonly referred to up there. He made his way and was shown into Smith's inner office. The governor waved at him and did not get up or shake hands, but motioned him to one of the armchairs on the other side of the desk.

Smith put down his cigar, called him by his last name, receiving a nod in return, and then said, "From the 6th AD, right?," and received another nod in return. "You won by six votes," the governor continued. Al Smith was later known to respond to the questions from reporters—after visiting his rival and by then president of the United States, Franklin Delano Roosevelt—when they asked him what he had managed to get the president to promise to New York State, "Did you ever try to nail a custard pie to the wall?"

This time his message was more succinct. He leaned forward, pointed at his visitor, and said, "Don't do it again," and dismissed him with a wave.

V   YOUR THIEVIN' SON

AN ITALIAN RESTAURANT within a couple of blocks of Tiffany's witnessed one of the more unusual exchanges between dining neighbors in Manhattan in the recent past. At a small table in a lightly populated restaurant at lunch sat two ladies dressed at Saks and coiffed at Elizabeth Arden, with tailored suits, upswept hair, and perfect nails. Past the empty table for two next to them were seated half a dozen men, neatly dressed, wearing work boots and with their hard hats on the floor next to their chairs.

The restaurant (no longer open) was named Vago, because the owner had been the maître d' at Quo Vadis, a famous Italian restaurant farther up on the East Side, and this place was supposed to be vaguely reminiscent of that one, possibly a joke only a native Italian could fully appreciate. Several doors down, a tall building was going up, and it was safe to conclude that these gentlemen were from the upper echelon of that project, possibly senior labor and management field people. In the background, you could just barely hear the steady drumming of large-scale construction machinery beavering away.

The women were talking about the difficulties of raising children in the City. The teenage son of one of them had taken to giving away his CDs to poor kids wherever he found them, to the point of shoplifting from one of the big stores to fulfill his sense of social mission. The boy had been nailed and was now working at the store to make amends and restitution. The waiter brought the fish special to both of the women, and they responded with an appropriate small and gentle noise.

At the men's table, a cell phone rang. One of the men picked it up and said, "Yeah? Okay. What's the problem?" At this point, one of the women remarked what a shame it was, how much she disliked it, when people talked on their cell phones in restaurants, and how inconsiderate it was to fellow diners. The man asked his caller to hold on for a second and, covering the mouthpiece with his hand, leaned in the direction of the two, saying, "I tell you what. What you do at your table, you and your thievin' son and everything, you do over there, okay? And what I do at my table, with all due respect, I do over here at my table. So excuse me, please, and enjoy your lunch by all means."

VI GIVE OR TAKE A BILLION

SEVERAL YEARS AGO, on a holiday trip back to Manhattan, I was early for lunch with a college friend—our lunch was at one and it was just noon—so I stopped at an ATM on Columbus Circle and walked up Broadway, looking for a dive bar that would produce a timely Bloody Mary. There are no dive bars within twenty blocks to the north and ten to the south, something I discovered without undertaking nearly that amount of research. The Bloodies still flourish, although in more upscale surroundings.

The first place I spotted was Gabriel's, five stars on the *Mobil Wine Guide*'s ratings posted under glass by the front door. I had eaten there several times and always been well pleased, so I plugged myself into a comfortable bar stool with a cushioned back and asked the short Hispanic bartender for my drink of choice. I was the sole customer at the bar, and probably in the restaurant, since noon meals in New York are traditionally at 12:30—to allow for all the contingencies that ceaselessly occur on the Magic Island, including the twelve phone calls that arrive between 12:10 and 12:25 most days.

The bartender disappeared, and a well-dressed gentleman of Caucasian persuasion approached me from behind the counter and offered me a menu. I explained, as I surveyed his Tattersall shirt, tweed jacket, and British-style club tie, that I was just having a quick one before meeting a college friend uptown for lunch. He asked me which restaurant and, when I told him, threw his hands up slightly, saying he lived a block away and loved it, so if I wasn't going to let him feed me at least I had shown good taste. We chuckled appropriately and he extended his hand, introducing himself as Gabriel—as in the restaurant's name—and asking me where I'd gone to college.

I don't often get asked that question, to be sure. Many friends say that, if you know me for more than ten minutes, I will have made you aware that I'm the first in my family to attend college, much less graduate, that I'm the secretary of my Princeton class, which also featured Bill Bradley, U.S. senator, Olympic and NBA champion, and Hall of Famer, and the man who should have been president instead of W (or Gore), and that Charlie Gibson, as nice and genuine a guy as you will ever meet, is a very casual friend of mine. My friends also say that when I stop this behavior they will start to believe I'm on the way to overcoming my lifelong insecurity and joining the human race. But in this case I was the one asked, so I focused on the question and the proper answer and left out the Jeopardy champion part (but not Bill or Charlie).

"We don't see Bill here so often these days," Gabriel responded. "He used to come in all the time with Herb Allen. You know, Allen & Co., down on Fifth above Cartier's and near St. Patrick's." I said I did know, had been there—although not to see Bill—and that word had it Herb had let Bill use his private jet when he made his presidential run. I added that I had donated to all Bill's campaigns, which enabled me to meet the Knick heroes of those championship teams, as well as Paul Simon. Gabe had met them also, at one time or another, but he asked me to remind Bill that he needed to renew his membership soon. We had another good chuckle, and the next thing I knew I was in possession of a second drink, on the house, since I had paid the original bartender for the first.

We chatted a bit about the restaurant business and other famous Princeton alums, and I told him one of my millions of stories about the Best Old Place of All, as we have dubbed it. This one was about Paul Sarbanes, the late U.S. senator and co-author of the Sarbanes-Oxley Act, which sought to clean up Wall Street and the mega-banks who brought about the Great Recession.

Sarbanes went to high school on the Eastern Shore of Maryland and was the son of a Greek immigrant who ran a popular restaurant there. A member of the local PU Schools Committee visited the high school's principal, saying the university was looking to broaden its student body in an attempt to break away from classes where all the members had gone to St. Grottlesex or its many rivals. He asked if there were any students that the—he almost said headmaster but corrected himself in mid-slip—principal might think qualified. This was in the fall of 1949. Sarbanes's name came up immediately.

It was the right move all around. Sarbanes won the Pyne Prize, the highest student award we have, was a Rhodes Scholar, over time became recognized as easily the brightest member of the United States Senate during his tenure, and wrote major legislation designed to protect the country and its citizens and not to advance special interests or repress some portion of those who live here and hope to enjoy its benefits and bounties.

When Senator Sarbanes—I'm almost finished, I said to Gabriel—was awarded the highest alumni award on Alumni Day, he told this story. His father's restaurant was closed on Monday, as many are, so when Paul was a freshman, Sarbanes the elder decided to drive up early Monday morning and bring his son some food, to supplement what our dining halls served to the freshman and sophomore classes.

This included a baked ham, Maryland style, criss-crossed with clove studs and a checkerboard pattern of knife cuts to let the fat run off more efficiently, with pineapple slices and a light honey glaze. The gratitude and appreciation he felt about the good fortune his son had been accorded also showed up in his thinking, so he prepared a second ham and brought it along, too. Early-morning traffic up from Maryland was light, and the Jersey Turnpike sped things along, so it was just after eight in the morning that Mr. Sarbanes knocked at the back door of Prospect, the home of the president of Princeton University—who was then Harold Dodds—was shown into the kitchen and given a cup of coffee, and took a seat at the kitchen table. President Dodds came down in his bathrobe and PJs in about five minutes. The men shook hands, Dodds grabbed a mug and filled it, and they talked for about an hour with great enthusiasm before Mr. Sarbanes excused himself to make the delivery to his pride and joy. Before he left, he received an invitation to return anytime, with or without the ceremonial ham, and those meetings continued about twice an academic year, until graduation.

Gabriel and I did everything but wipe away a tear, and for a moment it was as if those two from more than fifty years ago were embodied in the restaurateur and the Princeton man on the bar stool. Silence can indeed be golden, and so it was in that moment.

But this is also Manhattan, so after a short but respectful time, Gabriel said, "Okay, this might not match up, but I've got one for you. You know Eric Schmidt, the Google Alphabet guy, right?" I nodded energetically, noting that I'd heard him speak, knew he was a trustee and enormously smart, successful, and influential, and what else?

"Well, he's got a place, sort of a pied-à-terre, on top of the Trump Hotel right across the Circle here, had it for some time. And he comes in here from time to time to eat, but mostly he shows up around ten at night or a bit later. Always the same outfit, sleeveless cut-off sweatshirt, not Princeton but no designer stuff, either—you can't read the name that used to be on it. Running shorts and, if you notice, loafers with tape wrapped around the soles just before the arch. Always looks like he just took a shower, but forgot to comb his hair—probably too busy making sure he wipes his glasses clean. And he always sits at the very end, near the door, so he can look down along the bar and the customers seated there. We do a very nice late dinner crowd at the bar, mostly professional people and Lincoln Center audience types, so it's lively but not overdone, nice low steady murmur and the clinking and clanking you would expect.

"So this particular night, Eric is looking a bit more helter-skelter than he normally does. A good number of our customers are professional women, elegant, well dressed, hardworking, and happy to enjoy a good meal, probably on the company, by themselves and decompress before heading home for a quiet night's sleep. One of our regulars waves me over"—he did a sweet imitation of the Manhattan professional woman's discreet but definitive wave, and went on.

"She waves me down so she can whisper in my ear and says, 'Gabriel, that guy down at the end has a very piercing look from behind those glasses, doesn't he?' I say yes he does in a low voice and she says to me, 'Aren't you a little worried about him? He looks almost like he just crawled up out of the sewer, don't you think?' I grinned to myself and said I thought she might be judging him a little harshly. When she asked me, 'Really?,' I said, 'Let me put it this way—when he loses twenty-two of his twenty-four billion dollars, I'll probably revisit my opinion of him, but until then? I think I'm good.'"

You don't have to imagine what anecdote I greeted my college classmate with at lunch. One thing I did—Gabriel's story was perfect as it was and needed no garnish, but I saved for my friend that a mutual classmate of ours, who is also a trustee of PU, had told me that while watching him in trustee meetings, he had often observed that Eric's look from behind his specs was indeed extremely intense. So the details matched perfectly, as one would hope and expect.

VII FRONT TOOTH

THE FIRST TIME my front tooth died was in tenth grade, when Richard Jones, the center on our football team, went up against me in gym class for a rebound. His elbows spread out as if for a football block, and the left one nailed me. I flew into the air for a couple of seconds—I weighed 150 then and stood 6 foot 3, so I was easily airborne. By the time I came down the tooth was dead, the nerve crushed by the fulcrum of his leap. It turned black in about a day. The dentist said I needed a crown, which would involve drilling my tooth out, implanting a metal post, and creating a ceramic "cap" replica of what had been there before. As I write this, the tooth pulses, even though the nerve has been "dead" for fifty years.

That cap worked throughout college. When I came to New York, I played squash a lot with my college roommate. He's more of a tennis player—tennis being an arm game and squash a wrist game, essentially. On Valentine's Day he nicked me with a follow-through, just the merest touch of his racket on my tooth; I'm a mouth breather because of my broken nose. The impact popped the back of the cap off, although the front remained intact and in place for about five seconds. Then it fell on the white painted wooden floor of the squash court and fragmented. When I went home, I rang the doorbell instead of using my key, so I could see my wife's face when I said "Be My Valentine" with no front tooth.

Possibly there is something about holidays, because the next time was a Fourth of July barbecue I was hosting while I house-sat for the firm's senior partner—a little like a kid having a party when the parents are away. I was playing Frisbee on the sweep of grassy lawn alongside the brook and in front of the rose garden. The party was going great and the beer and wine were flowing. In this Arcadian New Jersey setting, the idea of a one-fingered catch of the Frisbee became essential. It flipped off my finger and zinged me in—now you get it for sure—a certain exposed spot—which I found in the grass with its back again missing.

Finally came the Christmas when my daughter was three. I was sitting on the floor amid the wrappings when she came running at me, total eye contact and Marilyn Monroe smile. I opened my arms to catch her, and she tripped on the rug. In front of her, stretched out like the payload in a missile, was a Christmas book with heavy reinforced cardboard pages of exactly the type you would give only to a small child. Kaboom!

In four hours we were due a hundred miles away for dinner at my wife's sister's house. I shoved the tooth back in and kept opening presents, eating cookies, and tamping it further back in with my tongue. I sat up on the couch to collect some paper and boxes and sneezed. The whole room was full of unwrapped presents and their former adornments. My throat felt like I might have swallowed the tooth, or at least that's what my head told me. Twenty extra-long minutes later I found it sticking to a gift tag and headed off to the dentist who covers for my guy when he's away. Later, only two hours behind schedule, we sat down for Christmas dinner and drank a toast to family and resilience, and to Richard Jones for his ultimately humorous elbow.

VIII SOMEWHERE BETWEEN PHILLY AND SICILY, THERE'S A PLACE FOR US

WELL ALONG in my professional career came a period when I was doing a lot of business travel that involved one- or two-night stays in the Southwest, West Coast, or Hawaii, with the result that my usually reliable sleep patterns became interrupted and erratic to the point of confusion and dishevelment. I tried tryptophan, a soporific that turkey contains, but then read something troubling about it that made me seek a substitute. Ambien had already proven to have disturbing side effects, and Dramamine and antihistamines were desiccating with a sort of hangover effect, in that they lasted too long to get me rapidly back on my regular workaday schedule. Then I read about natural melatonin, over the counter, and said to be the choice of airline pilots, an unpaid endorsement that resonated with me.

I tried it several times coming home on long flights and witnessed no untoward side effects. I'd had trouble falling asleep on planes even before the airlines reduced standard-sized seating to molecular dimensions, but using melatonin on the home leg overcame that problem, and the sleep on the plane compensated for the wakefulness on arrival, so things averaged out at an equilibrium I was comfortable with and that approximated my normal schedule.

After one trip home, however, I realized I had forgotten to take the pill on boarding, deep in thought as I was about a Phoenix Suns securitization that ultimately ran afoul of the secret playbook of the NBA Brass (a non-athletic team that wields enormous hidden power apparently exempt from outside authority of any kind). Bedraggled and sleep-starved as I was on arrival at my apartment, I pulled the bottle out of my medicine cabinet and tossed one down. I felt essentially refreshed, if a bit off center, awaking at my normal East Coast weekend get-up time.

I went right into my routine, quietly closing the door on my sleeping beauty, putting the coffee machine to work, and uncovering the cage and opening the door so that O'Neill, our pet cockatiel, could hop on my extended finger, then my shoulder, and assist in my floor exercises. O'Neill had that name because the sex of cockatiels (just as with infant parakeets) is virtually undeterminable. At the time, the food editor for the Sunday *Times* was Molly O'Neill, while her beloved and much-admired brother Paul had installed himself upon his arrival from Cincinnati as the Yankees' right fielder. So we had the name/sex issue covered.

O'Neill could ask if you were a happy camper, and after 9/11 the bird had learned to whistle the opening bars of "The Stars and Stripes Forever" in time for Christmas dinner, which involved my youngish kids and the near relations of my then Dearest One, in dramatic fashion. He waited until we were seated in the living room enjoying dessert, coffee, and after-dinner drinks, then left his cage, flew onto my extended, shoeless but not sockless right foot, and launched into song. Everyone stopped, amazed, and half the group said, "What was that!?," upon which O'Neill trilled it a second time as if in response. The record will show that he never, in fact, did that trick again, but he certainly came through big time when the chips were down. More recently, he had expanded his repertoire by marching up and down the foot of the bed while I did my morning RCAF set of exercises on the machine-made Astrakhan rug on the floor below it, randomly echoing numbers as I grunted them out.

That morning I did my exercises on the living room rug while the coffee brewed, and O'Neill marched along the side of the large, square coffee table, chipping in as he had learned to do. I always counted out loud as I did the forty push-ups and sit-ups, although not when I did the same number of back and front leg lifts, since those were pretty easy. Over a short time he had picked up some of the numbers, especially the longer words and most especially the ones toward the end of the sit-ups, the last exercise of the set. He would also anticipate some of his favorite numbers, which often came out "Seventeen, nineteen, twenty-five, twenty-six, thirty-seven, thirty-seven, thirty-seven, thirty-seven."

I puzzled over this for a while and concluded that as I approached the end the sit-ups became somewhat more difficult, so my counting out loud assumed a more and more distressed and emphatic tone and volume. All this was the case that morning, after which we proceeded to retrieve the paper from the hall, pour some coffee, defrost, toast, and butter a bagel (sesame today), and proceed to the dining table, where I went to work on the paper and ultimately the crossword, while O'Neill ravaged my bagel and flitted around the room, perching on the mantel, the bookcases, his cage, and sometimes the backs of chairs.

Halfway through the puzzle, and not, I believe, due to anything in it, I suddenly had to know the name of the capital of Sicily. This was an internal command, not something I had read or been thinking about otherwise. I pursued the source of this. I have an unusual memory, especially for trivia. If it's unimportant, I am almost sure to know it. A childhood full of moving almost every year, seventeen schools before college, and not many friends have meant that I will read anything. Encyclopedias, almanacs, dictionaries, and newspapers constituted most of my available material at home, along with six books of collected columns of the *New York Herald Tribune*'s longtime humorist (which I read at least five times each), my mother's women's magazines, and, lastly, cereal boxes.

What I came up with was to say to myself, "Boy, this Metamucil is really kicking my butt!" I corrected myself quickly to melatonin, but the road to Sicily's capital remained obscure. One of the few things I know is that fugitive memories are like people of the opposite gender: the more vigorously you pursue them, the faster they will put distance between themselves and you. So I went back to the puzzle, comfortable with the idea that the answer would be forthcoming, if not on my schedule.

Saturday's crossword is the hardest of the week, with Monday's being the easiest and each day's progressively more difficult. The Sunday one is big and has a theme, but it can be worn down in the two and a half hours of pro football that is consumed with time-outs, commercials, and halftime. This puzzle had its quixotries, but not more than normal, so I was nearly done when I felt like thinking about the Friday night fights at St. Nick's Arena (which I now know is on St. Nicholas Avenue in central Harlem) that I used to watch with my dad, who was a big fan of prizefighting.

That led me directly to memories of James Norris, president and CEO of the International Boxing Congress, or IBC, who was called to testify before Congress during the early days of network TV, in connection with match fixing and keeping certain fighters off the air unless they cut the IBC in on their earnings from the televised fights. Norris later went to prison, or at least was convicted and fined, and lost his nifty monopoly for good, although far from good for him. I then chuckled to myself as the name Whitey Bimstein came to me.

Whitey was a famous cut man, of indeterminate age, in the realm of boxing: a master of mixtures that could staunch bleeding and let his combatant continue without disqualification. He was noticeable on the screen because of his shock of white or ash-blond hair—they looked the same from our black-and-white vantage point on the couch—and because of his constant shaking of several stoppered bottles toward the end of the later rounds of fights. Then I sat up straight in my chair, due to remembering the name of Whitey's co-conspirator, a man whose face you only had to look at once to know his name was BLINKY PALERMO! So there it was. The last two clues of the puzzle would be easily plugged in when I got back around to them, but it was time for two things: first, to celebrate the success of my stratagem appropriately; and, second, to figure out why it had taken such a long and circuitous route to track my quarry to its lair. The second was more compelling, especially since the melatonin had possibly put me into such an obsessive-compulsive state.

After just the right amount of thinking and analysis, I concluded that the Palermo synapse in my memory had been appropriated away from the realm of geography at an early age by the fight game and the pleasant experiences of watching such odd (to me) scenes as those boxing matches on a screen that showed the activity, but had no real capacity to portray the power of the punches or the sweat flying off the bodies and faces of the contestants, much less the blood spattering the canvas and the spectators. To learn about Sicily and its capital, years later, was nothing more than a footnote to my close-up, but nevertheless distant, experience, a fairy tale but with real people, that played in our living room once a week.

Celebration remaining, and time having passed, I refreshed my own mug, poured a hot new one for the lady in waiting, and took it and the newspaper into the bedroom to find her having just awakened and happy to see me. In a while, O'Neill fluttered in and perched comfortably along the top of a picture frame on the slice of wall between the glass doors to our terrace and the bay windows around the seating area, with its view on this bright morning of the Hudson all the way across to the Bayonne Bridge—which glowed at night with a semicircle of emerald lights along the arch they hung from.

Saturday newspapers can be quickly read when there is other business to attend to and a homecoming to be celebrated, and one thing led, as it often does, to another. The act of love was, accordingly, well under way when I heard a brief beating of wings, and then felt the warm breath of the tiny bird deep between my legs as he shouted, "Thirty-seven, thirty-seven, thirty-seven, thirty-seven, thirty-seven . . ."

IX A TALE OF TWO BREWSKIES

I KNEW JODIE FOSTER would be great when she played the sister of a high school senior in San Fernando Valley whose family had recently moved there. To get in with the right crowd, she pretended to be a sophomore boy. Her best moment was when she asked her brother's friends, "Anybody up for a brewski?," then pounded her chest and launched a cosmically resonant belch.

Today I was remembering my time in Manhattan and two particularly memorable bars, one of which, on the West Side, had been a speakeasy during Prohibition and now had a neon sign in the window that said, "Home-Like Cooking." The other was on East 50th Street, half a block from the Waldorf in a medium-priced hotel whose ownership and decor seemed to change yearly. Joel, who bartended at both places, had a PhD from Rutgers in theater. When he wasn't working at either, he directed plays Off-Broadway and ended up managing a bar in deepest, darkest Chelsea that was owned by Michael Imperioli, the actor who played the legendary "Christopha!" on *The Sopranos*.

The bar on the West Side, at 73rd and Amsterdam, had been around forever and was neatly situated to host the Allman Brothers during their annual month-long gig at the Beacon Theater. The establishment's most famous story was about a regular who went by "Mumbles" and could almost always be found there during the many hours it was open. Once, when the owner had to escort a longtime patron who needed help navigating the path to his apartment on the lowest floor of a brownstone sixty feet away, the owner told Mumbles, then the only other patron in attendance, that he was in charge, and that in the unlikely event something happened that he couldn't handle he was to call nine eleven and turn it over immediately to the cops. Mumbles rubbed his face vigorously, it being not far from 2 a.m., and looked credulously at the owner, saying, "Wait a min, Scottie— there's no eleven on a telephone!"

I came in there around ten or so one weekday evening and spotted Laurence Fishburne, the actor in *Apocalypse Now* and *Matrix*, among others, toward the back, chatting with a couple of the locals. Pointing that way, I asked the bartender if that was who I thought it was, and he confirmed it, urging "Go on down. He's very friendly. He's rehearsing for *Othello* on Broadway." I did as indicated and ended up sitting next to him, whereupon he turned to me, stuck out his hand, and said something like "Welcome, Pilgrim, grab a seat." Not to be outdone, I responded, "You know, you're instantly recognizable." He held my hand long enough to say, "Well, just call me Instantly then," and let it go with a laugh.

We talked about his rehearsals and, because the Mets were on the TV toward the end of a West Coast night game, we found them to be his team, as they were mine. It turned out he had been born and raised in Queens, and although he lived in L.A. could never root for anybody else. The reason was simple. He had been eight years old when the Miracle Mets won the World Series, and lived not far away from the stadium and the endless number of body shops that lined the streets on the far side of the outfield, opposite the subway. He remembered people storming the field after the final game, grabbing handfuls of sod, and stuffing it in D'Agostino grocery bags. The other thing I will never forget is that what got him the most was when he looked up at the sky and saw it was "A Perfect Mets' Blue!"

East 50th Street held a tapas bar with two bartenders: my friend Joel with the Rutgers sheepskin and a gorgeous young blonde who seemed to have something going with the manager, so she was as fresh as fresh could be due to nobody daring to mess with her. She immediately endeared herself to me by noting that when she called her mom and told her about the job, her mom misunderstood and screamed out, "A topless bar!? You can't work in a place like that!" The two bartenders kept up a lively patter with a lot of humor and some Nichols and May bits they had memorized for fun. Like everyone else in New York, they were really aspiring actors just trying to earn enough for bed and board and a shot at stardom.

The bar décor involved an elaborate overhead set of coffered mirrors, with a sort of short mirrored curtain across the top, no longer than ten inches, all encased with a silvery soldered material that looked like fudge that had been slapped on to secure it and then hardened and silvered up. Because of the angles involved at the top, you could look up and in the mirror see someone sitting next to you or across the way. The blonde had gone to my high school in northern Virginia and played saxophone with the school band in the White House for Reagan, but we forgave her for that. One day I looked up into one of those mirrors and saw her left profile while I was looking at the right one there in front of me. Suddenly it hit me. I looked at her and said. "Okay, I get it. Are you the Good Sharon Stone?" She responded with a cheery yes but then immediately turned serious and leaned toward me, noting, "But I'm also the Bad Sharon Stone, because I'm a Gemini, and so I gotta be US!"

Eventually, word about the place got around and, like Yogi Berra said, nobody went there anymore because it was too crowded. One Friday, months later, I had a party invitation up on the East Side, decided to stop in, and found Joel standing at the bar. The blonde had been gone a while, he said, off to Miami with the manager when the hotel changed hands again. We speculated whether that whole caper was some kind of money-laundering "wash sale," as the tax code calls them, and shook our heads because we really couldn't say. I started to sit down and order a drink when Joel put up his hand and said, "Not today, Mike. No time to shoot the breeze whatsoever."

I got a puzzled look on my face like "Don't you like me anymore because I'm not around so much?" (I had moved to a downtown firm three months earlier.) But he pointed to a largish group of women around a table in the window alcove next to the door and explained, "That's a retirement party over there. They've been packing it away for three hours straight. Now they're taking their party out to dinner somewhere and just asked for separate checks!" I'm sorry to say I never saw Joel again, but I'm sure he worked it out, however long it took. He was a very solid guy and remarkably even-tempered, which I guess you need to be in that line of work.

X ROYALTY IN HIGH RELIEF

MY DAUGHTER spent the summer after college graduation on the beaches of various Aegean islands with her Italian boyfriend—nude beaches, it would seem. In mid-August they found a rocky strand reachable only by ferry, and unpopulated because it contained no fresh water. Sweating through every pore, they descended one morning from the hillside campsite, where they'd slept, onto an unoccupied stretch of gorgeous beach.

As they emerged from their refreshing dip, suit-less in the extreme, they noticed a giant yacht, with a sailboat winched up on its stern and various dinghies alongside. They also observed a host of Royal Marines buzz ashore in several black rubber, motorized craft and proceed to set up cabanas, deck chairs, an open tent with several tables, and coolers obviously meant to hold liquid and solid refreshments. The next wave then landed, including the personages of Her Majesty the Queen, Princes Philip, Charles, William, and Harry, and associated young lovelies in bikinis, not including the then Camilla Parker Bowles.

My daughter and her boyfriend stayed on their end of the beach, the Royals on theirs, but one of the rubber boats soon arrived with two Royal Marines in it, and one hopped out with a small canvas bag. "You know who that is, I suppose?" he asked and/or stated, and they nodded, allowing him to remark that the Family gets very little "priv-acy" and would appreciate their displacing themselves around that point over there so as to cease being visible, with the annoying part being unspoken but clearly implied. He handed them the bag, saying "Compliments of Her Majesty," then headed back to his boat and on to the Royal encampment. They peered (pun intended) inside and saw two frosty Heinekens with the caps removed therefrom, noted that the bag had no logo on it, and trundled off as requested.

At the time I learned of this incident, I was cultivating an English client who owned water parks in the United States and a chain of beauty establishments selling his personal brand of associated products in Southeast Asia. He was a good friend of President Reagan, lived in L.A., and stayed at the St. Regis when in New York. One day I was enjoying lunch in his suite and decided to entertain him with my daughter's story. As an eternal embellisher, I decided to embroider the tale by turning those two bottles into a six-pack, but he stopped me in mid-sentence to observe that I must be making that part up, since that many beers were entirely beyond that family's capacity for generosity. So I confessed error and have stuck ever since to the naked truth, at least in that case.

XI "THAT'S DIFFERENT"

DURING LAW SCHOOL, a good deal of my decision not to become a courtroom lawyer or litigator was driven by the fact that I found them generally obnoxious and overbearing, as well as imbued with a worldview that encompassed only win/lose encounters. Their sense of a perfect world seemed to consist of a series of incidents in which they kicked someone hard in the groin, knocked them down, speared them in the chest and throat, and then stood over the corpse, pounding their chests and emitting Tarzan-like shrieks.

A little of that goes a long way, in my opinion, and as a firm believer in the superior beauty of win/win solutions, the last thing I wanted to do was to spend my life in the company of such primitive doowahs. But, as always, there was one exception that proved the rule. He became a close, lifelong friend, with whom I never had the misfortune to cross swords in a legal venue. For openers, he started his remarks at his sixtieth birthday party, to a large room full of legal and personal friends, by saying that he'd finally abandoned his youthful dream of winning a Nobel Prize, and was interrupted by one of his partners, saying to universal laughter that if there were a Nobel for interrogatories, he would have won it long ago.

Between the ages of four and six, I lived in Germany, where my father, a captain in the U.S. Army, was busily engaged in flushing out Russian operatives, as well as underground Nazis who had escaped the nets of the conquering forces and continued to conduct sabotage and espionage against the occupying powers. Starting in 1947, my family lived in an eighteen-room house with thirteen servants, including a chauffeur, a gardener/handyman, plus various cooks, chambermaids, and the like. I was the little prince of the kitchen, speaking German in one direction and English in the other, almost simultaneously, and the gardener and I often took long walks in the woods with our boxer dog, Argo. During that period, there were still people in Germany starving to death and work was difficult to find, so these jobs were precious to our staff. During our walks, we would pass from time to time an area surrounded by ten-foot-high steel fencing, with razor ribbon along the top and Quonset huts inside, peopled by sad-looking individuals in heavy coats and parkas, with their hands in their pockets, not appearing to be doing much of anything.

These were displaced persons from the war; refugees was the term then. As I learned during law school, my friend Marty had been in that very camp with his family while I was on the outside living in considerable comfort. They would ultimately immigrate to New York City, where he, as the oldest child and the best English speaker, would lead his parents and younger brother and sister through the mysteries of the subway system, developing an authoritative manner that would suit him well in later life.

Marty was an outstanding student with a prodigious memory. When he later became a partner in a prestigious Manhattan law firm, he told me that part of what enabled him to succeed was that he had essentially memorized every document in each case he tried. He also let me in on the litigator's trick, when challenged by the judge or the opposition to provide a legal authority or precedent for his position, of saying, "The McWithers case sets that position forth undeniably, Your Honor." Then he would send his junior lawyer back to find the case that actually did support the argument, because there always is such a case, somewhere, the law being the jumble it is. Someone would then call the judge, and his adversary, and provide the citation, along with an apology for having misstated the name of the case. When he called me with the news of his promotion to partnership, he started the conversation—after addressing me by last name in the tried-and-true Ivy League manner—with the famous Nixonian words "The long national nightmare is over." To be sure. When I asked him, some years later, about how the oral argument in the Supreme Court had gone in a case he was involved with, he simply said, "Well, when Justice Goldberg got us lost on the way to the Supreme Court, I had a feeling it was not going to be our day. I was right about that, for whatever that may be worth."

Once during dinner at his house, I paused the lively conversation to observe that, in what I hoped would be the long period of time we would be friends, the discussion would be both more pleasant and proceed more efficiently if he started restraining his habit of responding to everything I said with "You're wrong." He disputed that, of course, and I barked, "See what I mean? There you go again." He turned to his wife for support, and she said, "Mike's right. You do that all the time, to everybody." He paused for a moment, put his hands in front of him in a kind of supplicatory gesture, and said, "But, but, that's different." Who could argue with that?

On another occasion we were having lunch, and I asked if they were planning any trips in the near future. He indicated that they were going to Taiwan very soon. "Business or pleasure?" I queried, not being familiar enough with Taiwan to offer anything more specific. A slightly disdainful expression occupied his face for the long moment it took me to say, "Oh, I get it. Nobody goes to Taiwan for pleasure, right?" and got the nod he had been waiting to give. I asked what the case was about, if he could tell me. He responded by asking if I was familiar with an insider trading case involving a sort of mogul whose last name was Lee, and I excitedly exclaimed, "Lee? You've got Lee?" only to be met with the response of "I wish I had Lee. My guy's innocent!"

To round out the portrait, Marty is an extremely generous person, to our law school and many other worthy charities, and gives anonymously, because Maimonides taught that the proper purpose of giving is not to polish one's reputation, but to do good humbly and not proudly.

Marty also has a fine sense of humor, as demonstrated by the following story. At one time he decided to study the cello, as a diversion from his intense focus on the law and with the thought, when he became adequately proficient, of renting a hall and inviting his family, friends, and legal associates to a recital. This plan never eventuated, but he did take lessons for several years and went for summers to an upstate college where a music camp was conducted, mostly for younger students but also for a few more advanced in years. His one problem was that he has always been an early riser, while the youngsters tended to stay up late and the breakfast facilities thus didn't open until around 8 a.m., so he had to bring his own coffeemaker. And he found it difficult to get to sleep because of the noise from the younger students, before midnight and even after.

His ever-resourceful wife tried to help solve this problem by purchasing for him a proper black sleep mask. The night before she was to drive him up to the college, he was packing and she was making a lunch for them in the kitchen. She heard his voice behind her, and when she turned around he was standing there, wearing nothing but the sleep mask and reciting verbatim the introduction that followed the William Tell Overture at the beginning of each episode of *The Lone Ranger*—pow pow (imitating a two-gun draw and shooting), "Hi-ho, Silver! A fiery horse with the speed of light, a cloud of dust and a hearty 'Hi-ho, Silver!'—The Lone Ranger! Hi-ho, Silver, away! With his faithful Indian companion, Tonto, the daring and resourceful masked rider of the plains led the fight for law and order in the early West. Return with us now to those thrilling days of yesteryear. The Lone Ranger rides again!"

Marty also hosted the most nickel-and-dime poker games

ever held in Manhattan, I believe once a month, with current and former lawyers from his firm, including judges, all mining the same vein of humor. Once, in a game of "Pass the Trash," I was called by another player. My response was "Eights," Pass the Trash being a game that strongly resembles its name. We were the last two in the hand. My neighbor said, "I hope that wasn't plural." Finally—and these, I will admit, were all litigators—one guy, before removing his coat and loosening his tie, told us we had missed a great scene in federal court that day where he was trying a securities case, which he hoped and prayed made it into the transcript.

"So I'm cross-examining this witness, and the judge asks me why I'm pursuing this line of questioning, and I respond that if he knows the Consolidated Ute Supreme Court case, he'll understand." Marty immediately asked if this was a McWithers move and was waved off, to a general round of laughter. The guy continued, "Then the court reporter says, 'Ute?' and I say back, 'Yes, Ute,' and the judge says, 'What is this? *My Cousin Vinnie?*'"

There can be fun in the law, at least after hours.

XII SATURDAY BRUNCH IN THE HEART OF BERGEN COUNTY

MOST PEOPLE on our street don't know each other except through kids or dogs. We're all relatively new and from different places, some from around this town and some from everywhere else. Everyone lives their lives and plays in parallel. We love our kids and we love our pooches, neither of those involving direct love between a given person and another, which would be prohibited in these monogamous communities, because of fear of the straying of the straight ones, or the crossing of the street by those who aren't as straight as they would like others to think. But at a remove, through the medium of offspring or beloved canine companions, we can radiate and receive that warmth.

We invite our immediate neighbors, and maybe the people one house farther down, to parties we give outside. They reciprocate. The kid/dog thing, upon the acquisition of our beloved rescue dog Lady Gwendolyn the dachshund, expands that mode to across and up and down the street, so in a superficial sense we have a neighborhood, and we certainly have people talking to each other across leashes and waiting at school bus stops. I got the word on the chiropractor from the Dominican Republic across the street getting it on with his assistant—the result was a beautiful, deep brown Beamer convertible he had to buy his wife to get her to stay. Oddly, their chocolate Lab is named Godiva, and all the ladies were in on the story. That's communication.

My next-door neighbor is Hungarian, and his wife is Latina. They have a border collie. He and I meet over the garbage and he says to me, "You know how on TV you see this guy with his wife in the background, standing in front of his house in a nice, clean shirt, and he says, 'He always seemed like a nice, happy guy, I can't imagine what would make him do a thing like that.' Well, amigo, you might be needing that shirt a little later in the day if it keeps going where she's pushing it, you know what I mean?" "My good friend," I say, "come on down to my basement and let me get you a cold one. Then you can tell me how to set up my work tool bench and remember how to breathe easy." Rescue squad and a long cool schmooze goes good distance as part of any community.

Best of all was the dog birthday party without the kids. The owners of big Newfie down the block, who has hip displasia and sits prominently on the front stoop, decided to celebrate his birthday with a neighborhood get-together. About a dozen couples converged around two on a Saturday afternoon at Eiffel's house, where he was, as usual, taking up most of the doorway. Through the house and onto the back patio, the path led to a bar and umbrella tables. On the way I noticed an older gent in the small library, focused on the TV. His ex-wife was in the back and they have agreed to never be in the same space, open or closed, again—parents of the wife of the house, Eiffel's mom, Gina.

If you follow this, Gina's mom, the one who doesn't speak to her ex, proved to be Gloria, and she was well into the fun by the time I arrived. The punch was high-octane—that part of the taste stood out. The magic moment came during our conversation when she looked at me at the same moment the clouds parted, so that a shaft of light fell across her face. "You know," I said, "you have the most beautiful green eyes! Wow!"

"Oh," she said, "Thank you so much. You remind me so much of my second husband—my true love—I miss him so much—he used to say that, something like that. Do you like them? Are you telling me the truth?" It was easy to be honest. The effect of the moment had been kaleidoscopic and incandescent.

"He was such a wonderful man," she went on. "Jewish, but he liked it. He sure did. Twice a day and three times on Sundays. Those Sundays were a workout!" The guys were in front of the garage, around the keg, talking baseball. I later learned that the discussion among the women across the patio had been about what your dog does while you're trying to have sex. Some like to watch, and some like to join. That kind of closeness is what makes a development into a neighborhood.

XIII READIN', WRITIN', AND 'RITHMATIC

PEOPLE CONSTANTLY DENY the benefits of college education, especially liberal arts and humanities studies in the Ivy League or similar highly rated institutes. Such comments usually come from those schools' own graduates, but who could be better qualified? That, in itself, is your first clue. Pay attention, and there might be more for you. We all know that all figures lie, and liars figure. We also know that a story or two, of the right sort, are worth any number of algorithms, which in fact is what any number of algorithms in essence are. I'll settle for two similar stories, because two is my favorite prime number, the only even one, so you're essentially obliged to trust it. Nor is it the loneliest number, as "one" comes to know. It's also not the infamous "scientific sample of one," which is to cite some anomaly that portrays your case as representing all available possibilities, but restricts its sample, and thus yours, to the One the other side will like least. But enough theorizing.

Two good friends of mine went to very prestigious universities. One, my best friend in high school, majored in English and obtained a PhD in that subject, and the other was a history major who has climbed the highest mountain on each continent except Antarctica. Both of them were of draft age during the Vietnam War. They both lived in prosperous suburbs of Washington, D.C., one on each side of the Potomac. Both also went into the Peace Corps after graduation from college, and when they came home, both found notices to report for induction into the United States Army. Each complied, served two years, and received an honorable discharge.

You might think it would be hard to show how these facts support my premise, but check this out. Both are named Dave, so to distinguish them I will refer to them as Abe (for Able) and Baker (for obvious reasons). Abe is one year older, but that makes no never mind in this situation.

Abe came from a politically liberal family. When drafted, he was sent to Fort Bragg, North Carolina, for basic infantry training and stayed for advanced infantry training. (You die sooner.) During the second part of that, he helped found an antiwar coffeehouse just outside the main gates of Fort Bragg. While I was studying for the bar exam after law school, I received a visit from an FBI agent, who took off his hat as he sat down, then took out his notebook and asked if he could ask me a few questions about Abe, to which I said of course.

The reason, he explained, was that Abe was being considered for a position of trust and confidence with the United States government, and so this was a standard background check. The interview went on for about half an hour, and after a while I put together the pattern of his questions, so that for each one that required a factual answer, the next one veered into opinion territory, specifically relating to Abe's loyalty to our country, his membership in prohibited political groups, any expressions of antipathy toward "our country's position on the war," and whether he had been known to have written or spoken anything that someone might consider treasonous.

Innocent as I have always been of the evil and deceit that characterizes our species—a friend of mine claims that, because of Eve, every human being has a worm in his apple and that's just for starters—I caught onto his game. Abe was being considered for a broadly and horizontally striped suit in which he would find it easy to grab a piece of wall, spread 'em, and let his pants get pulled down so the people empowered by law to do so could poke up inside him and see if he was concealing contra- band such as dynamite or automatic weapons. I didn't see much trust or confidence anywhere near that particular MOS (military occupational specialty).

The oddest or most ironic thing about the situation was that Abe's family was a paragon of loyalty to a much higher level of American patriotism than anyone else I had ever met. They loved this country more for what it stood for and could stand for than just about anyone I knew. I respected and admired them so much that in high school I even prayed I would get adopted into Abe's family—without anything bad happening to my par- ents, of course—but it would have been such an obvious step up it was hard not to want it very badly. So without even a whiff of "perjury" or "making false statements to an officer of the law," I could tell the total truth and give this jerk-off a notebook full of rapturous praise for his prospective jailbird, and because I was a liberal arts student and a prospective lawyer, I could cast my praise in the very language of our founding documents and patriotic speeches.

Abe didn't think it was so funny when I called him—I knew better than to write him, and arranged through his parents to talk directly. I was dead-on in my analysis, but to him it was far from a laugher, because he had already gotten unequivocal warnings that they wanted badly to make an example of him, and send him, Dreyfus-like, to Leavenworth for long enough to grind his bones to make their bread.

I won't claim any credit for what happened, because of the high regard I have always had for Abe. So I'm sure that his being reclassified from a grunt made of cannon fodder for Vietcong am- bushers into a clerk-typist headed for Germany with a role to help put out the base newspaper was his doing, not mine. The Army is good at very few things, but one of them is removing a square peg from a round hole. They knew that sending Abe to 'Nam would not remove the danger of his undermining morale or, since he was a plausible Communist, at least in their eyes, starting to spy for the other team. They knew as well that he'd been to college, that he could type and organize paperwork, and that Germany was on the other side of the globe from Southeast Asia.

I was delighted with the result. He received an honorable discharge, got his PhD, taught literature in college, became the head of the department, and wrote a textbook that is widely used today, even after his retirement. He also has spent a lot of time enjoying Fulbright grants to teach about our country and study other cultures all over the world, entirely on the taxpayer's nickel.

I would say, "Beat that!" or "Top that!" but I will spare you the effort and give you Dave #2, AKA or better known as (BKA) Baker.

I learned Baker's story later. We went to college together yet never met. When he caught up with me, the comparison with Abe proved compelling, and that, in part, is why I argue for a "liberal" education. Some single-digit-IQ preacher in Ohio recently told his congregation to make sure they never sent a child to a place that would teach the child anything the parents didn't already know. I, for one, also liberally educated, disagree.

Baker did the same as Abe, up to a point: liberal arts, Peace Corps, draft notice upon completing "Government Service," and off to Fort Dix, New Jersey. Baker, for reasons he alone knows, was confident he would survive. Among young people who fail to gain a liberal arts degree, this is rare, because you are stuck with one of only two stories (remember the number two, please)—the life you're living or the one in which the numbers have been cooked to show the result the prof wants, and will earn you a small job in a big operation where your life, or anything about you, is automatically referred to HR. So confidence is rarely available in situations where you have no foundation such as experience in the real world or education.

But Baker sits tight, is cool, and thinks about the mountains he will climb in years to come. He doesn't qualify for advanced infantry training, but he does come down with food poisoning at the mess tent (like military music and military intelligence, one of the few perfect oxymorons). He gets sent off to the infirmary for a couple of days, and when he comes back—ta da—his whole basic training unit has shipped out for the Big Muddy, thereby gaining the opportunity to come home one of two ways, and no one needs instruction on what they were. Emphasis on were.

The sergeant who runs the barracks looks at him and asks what he's doing here. He reminds Sarge that he had been sent to the infirmary, taken in a stretcher by medics, because he was puking his guts out and shitting his brains out. He thinks for a moment about noting that each of those expressions is not literally true, but he clams up, awaiting further developments.

Sarge looks at him again and asks if he can type. Says to him, straight out, didn't you go to college and learn typing? He acknowledges those facts, and Sarge takes a deep breath, smiles, and says that all these forms he's got to fill out from Baker's bunch of so-called soldiers are eating him alive, because he never went to any GD college and he cannot f—— type! Note that the number of recruits he "processed" octupled during a short span of time.

Being as the two of them are enlisted and non-com Army people, respectively, career and draftee, they do not shake hands, but they do agree that until the next batch comes through and finishes their preparation for the great beyond—whatever its terms might ultimately be—if Baker types his ass off and keeps in shape and his head down, no one will make a fuss, and everybody will do all right in the meantime.

Basic training lasts six weeks. After about three weeks, Sarge is playing pool and buying beers at the NCO club with an unusually cheerful mien. The other NCOs buy him more beers and find out that Baker is his joy boy: college, some kind of Ivy League, and can type like Rafer Johnson can throw the Olympic javelin.

Within a day or two, word reaches the Colonel, whose assistants are NCOs, that Sarge has a guy salted away in his barracks who is a world-champion typist and he's keeping him all to himself! Colonel goes down to investigate, and they agree in almost no time at all that Baker belongs at HQ, not in some outlying barracks where the Army cannot make the best of use of him in the National Interest. No hard feelings, and Sarge, you know you got a lot of mileage out of this boy like he was a friggin' Jaguar XKE, so no tears and thanks for the memories.

Baker and the Big Man hit it off incredibly well. Next thing you know, Baker is caddying for the Colonel on his twice-a-week golf game, and they are talking about all kinds of stuff, both real and unreal, laughing so hard you can hear them a fairway or two away.

But no one says anything about that, since, if you know one thing, it's not to cross the Colonel. How do you think he got there? By being anybody's best friend for more than five minutes? Think again.

Close as they are, and lonely as colonels who are CEOs (or any CEO as such) can be, the Colonel lets Baker in on a secret, which is that he cannot hold him here at Dix any longer. All the options have been exercised and all the alternatives have been put on direct current, so there is just one way out.

Promotion! He tells Baker he is promoting him, while changing his MOS, which does happen more than you might think, since the U.S. Army does need flexibility and this is about all they've ever been able to think of and get done. Baker becomes a Clerk-Typist First Class, a separate category but not that much unlike good old Abe's previous road to both safety and lederhosen.

But to confirm this promotion, Baker needs to go to Fort Benjamin Harrison, in Indiana, where the Army sends guys who can really, really type and file! Baker did more filing for his senior thesis at a fine institution of learning than he ever comes close to at Fort BH, frequently referred to as Fort BJ because it was a soft post near a lot of women's colleges.

Like many graduates of rigorous training such as his alma mater, Baker comes in first in his class, and nobody minds, because they saw him at work, a number of them exclaiming "Well, he did go to some college," and he rides out to his next assignment.

By this time, Baker's enlistment is half over. He gets sent to Los Alamos, where the Army needs someone to type up the notes of General Groves, the head of the Manhattan Project, the boss of Oppenheimer, Fermi, von Neumann, Feynman, and hundreds of other geniuses—because Groves was a military man, and this is still a military project. Groves is now part of history, front-page, world-class history, and don't forget what Baker majored in. Not accounting, not farming, not even marine biology or entrepreneurship.

Please follow this: the liberal arts major, although from a very good institution of higher learning, was one night away from being turned into something dead and gone. Due to various factors, including getting sick on the food afforded his classification, he avoided that fate, met lots of interesting people, had the leisure to translate the handwriting of a man in charge of a thousand men far smarter than he was, who had to deliver a product he never really understood very much about. Baker, almost undoubtedly, had a much better time on the Manhattan Project transcription than did General Groves, although Groves got a nice medal. But so did Baker, as well as an honorable discharge and the wherewithal to get his MBA from Stanford, another one of those highfalutin spots some say are not worth the money. But he did then make a ton of money, go mountain climbing to his heart's content (although he ultimately needed titanium balls in both knee joints), and end up living in beautiful Santiago, Chile, within view of the Andes, with an American passport.

The secret, of course, is imagination, flexibility, and patience. Both my subjects had all that, along with a college degree ultimately worth freedom, avoidance of jail and wartime suffering, etc. That's part one, if that's not enough for you.

Part two is best explained by my book club of six over-seventy-year-old guys who have similar backgrounds and (of course) degrees from similar institutions. It's a great bunch, assembled by one of our number several years ago. We meet monthly, read serious books that are not mass-market or genre-icious, have lunch, and talk for a long and worthwhile time. The first time we met, we were perfect gentlemen. We talked a little about ourselves but mostly asked questions about each other, for information and glad-handing, so everyone understood how important everyone else was in their own, and our, eyes.

By the second meeting, we tried a little bit of that small talk to begin with—BTW, most of us don't drink anymore, or at least not there. But within almost no time after the opening chit-chat, the testosterone emerged, bright-eyed and bushy-tailed. We started talking Board Scores, as in PSATs, SATs, LSATs, GREs, GPAs, and the like. You could hear a "whoosh" shoot through the room. These guys majored in one pure science or another, or else politics, history, engineering, usw. (German for etc.). I majored in English literature. The essence of literature is telling the false from the true, combining them in different and amazing ways, and considering how and why one thing can be false and its virtual twin true, and why things can often look more real upside down than they do right side up. Fun stuff like that.

I enjoyed this and, to be honest, giggled inside about this thing that guys cannot help but do. I waited for everyone to wave their you-know-what's to the amazement and adoration of each other, and then I threw in, casually, my own numbers. These were not real numbers, but numbers derived from what numbers I had to beat, and so they did. Because nobody knows "The Truth" and never will, which is what one learns if you pay attention in the courses I took and loved. And still do.

XIV BROTHER ACT

FAMILIES of extremely successful siblings have always been a topic of interest for me. Take Whitey Bulger, New England crime kingpin, and his brother Bill, who was the head of the Massachusetts legislature; Bruce (a legend on Wall Street nicknamed "Bid 'em up Bruce") and Wendy (Pulitzer Prize–winning playwright) Wasserstein; Rahm Emanuel (Obama chief of staff and mayor of Chicago) and his brothers Ari (big-time Hollywood agent and model for the *Entourage* series on HBO) and Ezekiel (leading bioethicist and adviser to the Obama administration on health policy); and the Breyer brothers (Stephen of the Supreme Court and his sibling, Charles, who is probably the most widely admired living federal judge not on the Supreme Court)—to name a few.

What happened in their families to cause more than one child to rise to special achievement and recognition? The Harbaughs, Jim and John, coached against each other in a Super Bowl, but anyone who put his money on the younger of the two, presumably due to his All-American status versus his brother's lesser success on the field, would have been better off eating it. Those rivalries are done, once and for all, at an early age, and even though that Super Bowl came down to the last play, the older brother won, as he had done in one-on-one situations throughout their lives. Jonas Salk of the polio vaccine and his brother Lee, who revolutionized dealing with infants and whose wisdom I was fortunate enough to receive as a young father, are another pair with happier results for humankind. Shirley MacLaine and Warren Beatty? What better pair on which to rest my case?

But not yet. Athletic dynasties abound, as in DiMaggio, Griffey, Fielder (both great long-ball specialists, perfectly enough, even though they haven't spoken for years), Norton (dad should have gotten the decision over Ali, while son won numerous Super Bowls and made a career in NFL coaching—they also don't speak) and the endless skein of Boones in baseball, unto the third generation. Intelligence and quick-twitch muscle reflexes undoubtedly play central parts in their respective domains, and some doubt must exist respecting any single answer to this question, although that still doesn't make it unworthy of investigation and analysis.

It is hard to imagine, but many prosperous parents these days purport to scheme up some version of this for their offspring, although a more long-standing and enduring family culture will often be at the heart of this unusual phenomenon. Take the Adams family, as in John, John Quincy, Charles Francis, Henry, and more, along a number of generations, or the James family, in which Alice, Henry, and William—at different times, but nevertheless—were acclaimed as revolutionary, insightful geniuses. As in any derby, many may answer the call to the post, especially in this new gilded age of billionaires and increasing segregation by economic status and educational credentials. As the first in my family to graduate from college, I cannot assert a hereditary insight into how such things occur, although my son got into Yale and my daughter taught me the Phi Beta Kappa handshake.

My closest encounter with such a family involved two brothers who practiced law with two substantial Wall Street firms (no longer extant), which at one time occupied extremely high floors in One Chase Manhattan Plaza. That building was the cornerstone of Wall Street's architectural and commercial revival when the juice started flowing up into Midtown—its similarity to the United Nations Secretariat Building signaled that it was unmistakably by Gordon Bunshaft of Skidmore, Owings & Merrill (which sounds like a law firm, on top of everything else). The building once was the address of seven of the top fifteen law firms in the city. All of these were WASP firms, no Jews, thanks anyway. David Rockefeller, CEO of Chase, was the landlord, and his family's firm roosted on floors forty-five through forty-seven. That mother lode of intelligence and breeding may well have contained another set of brothers comparable to these two, but, to paraphrase the one and only Bartleby the Scrivener, I prefer not to think so.

To give you a bit of the brothers' background, both parents were attorneys, father a federal judge in Manhattan and mother one of the earliest female members of the New York Bar. The two sons were not close in age but followed similar paths: New York private schools, New England prep schools, Yale or Harvard, then Yale Law School. There the similarities end.

Brother A—let's call him Reginald A, because in his bios his "nickname" is Reginald A. The Getty Archive's only image of him shows him in a three-piece suit and smoking a long-stemmed brier pipe, smiling behind his horn-rimmed glasses. His office, on the fifty-fifth floor of One Chase, looks north and is very spare. He faces away from the nearby back window, looking inward, behind which lay a huge slice of low-rise housing and then the Empire State, Chrysler, and Rockefeller Center buildings. You get the sense you are looking down on that spectacular panoply, in front of which, dramatically backlit, he sits.

The setting consists of a large Persian rug in red, yellow, and brown, with some black accents, which happen to be the same colors that adorn the backs of the bound law reports occupying floor-to-ceiling sets of bookshelves on the east and west walls, ending at the window. Anyone involved in law immediately recognizes the tomes as the *Federal Reporter* series, of which there are a lot of volumes, containing all the federal cases of the era. The desk has no drawers except perhaps a central one, so you can see the rug and his legs as he sits waiting for you. No papers are in sight, even in front of him.

He welcomes you, bids you sit in one of the visitors' chairs on the south side of the desk, and asks if you know anything about him. Having done your homework, you know that at a young age he was made the head of the antitrust branch of the Justice Department and profiled in *Fortune* magazine with a photograph of him standing on the steps of the Supreme Court. He congratulates you on your answer, which feels like a verbalized pat on your back, then pulls out what can only be your résumé and transcript from a folder on his blotter. A few questions follow.

He asks if you know a certain fellow student, a year ahead of you, who clerked at his firm the year before and was second in his class at the law school all three of you attended. You know the name but nothing more. He leans forward, repeats the other student's class standing, and says what a pleasure, indeed almost a privilege, it had been to work with that young fellow, and even more delightful that he would be returning after graduation to keep working with your host. You nod and smile. He tells you about the great trip they took to Calgary on a case last summer, and how terrific it was to be able to spend not only a working day, but also a social evening, with someone who possessed an intellect that put him second in his law school class.

Then comes the curve ball, the question of whether you haven't been wishing that you yourself were second in your class, considering what a great career ahead of you that would betoken. You smile again, nod, and say you guess so. He snorts, replying, "Yes, I would think you would, wouldn't you. Too bad it's not the case, though, isn't it? Too bad." He looks around the room as if suspecting that someone has violated the invisible "No Farting" sign and pushes his intercom button while picking up the phone to convey a message to the individual at the other end that he thinks we're done, and would she please summon the recruiting coordinator. You hope momentarily that when she comes in he will rip off her blouse, pull a cat-o'-nine-tails out of that middle drawer, and flog the bejesus out of her while you get to see her breasts bounce around. This fantasy, given your youth, starts to provide you with an untoward chubby, and you try (with only moderate success) to stifle a snort, which he doesn't respond to—because, in the most important sense, you are no longer there to him, and only he snorts.

I took a job with another firm in the building on a slightly lower floor and spent time on the Upper East Side visiting friends, so I continued to see Reginald A from time to time. He always wore a black bowler and generally carried an umbrella. I would smile at him in a friendly manner in our common elevator because I noticed that he didn't like it—he didn't know who I was, most likely because no one he didn't know should have any right whatsoever to smile his way, and he would never demean himself to ask the appropriate question, so he was stuck. On a fair number of occasions, I walked down the block in the evening past his brownstone. More often than not, I saw him through the central window of the parlor floor, spotlighted by his large desk lamp, poring over presumably legal papers with pen in hand. As the saying goes, that was all I knew and and all I needed to know.

Completely by chance, however, I did go to work for the firm where his somewhat younger brother was a partner. Since I accepted their offer of employment after my summer tryout, and stayed there quite a while, I spent a good deal more time with that brother. On one occasion, after I'd become a partner, I was accompanying the younger one to lunch when the older one hopped on our elevator just before the doors closed. They nodded to each other, standing side by side and never turning to face each other, as we all went down to the Plaza and half a block to the Downtown Association gentlemen's club. On the way down, my partner said, "How's she taking it?" A somber moment passed, then the emptiness was filled by a response of "Well enough, under the circumstances," with a rejoinder of

"Has to be pretty tough," and finally "Well, you know." We then got off and parted ways. I learned upon asking that this exchan-age concerned the recent death of a family housecat, and the subject more or less changed itself.

Richard, the younger brother, was known as Dick, and he seemed to have inherited all the humor that had passed down to his generation. He drove a fire-engine-red, 60s-style full-length Mercedes station wagon, not the SUV version, which was surely the only such ever registered in Manhattan. He also was wont to tell stories, like about how he and his wife were invited to a Hal-loween party, to come dressed as a famous couple, and therefore acquired lab coats from a physician whose offices were on the ground floor of their Madison Avenue residence, and went as Masters and Johnson. A good start, I thought.

I treasure the memory of one day about three years into my tenure there, when the '70s were getting some wind in their sails as to fashion, even on Wall Street. Based on considerable observation, I figured out two things that changed my life. First, I could wear Italian loafers instead of tie shoes, although I eschewed Gucci's as too obvious and common and opted for Bal-ly's—but only the Italian ones, not the Swiss version, because you want your shoes to have a friendly formality, not a haughty look.

Equally important, because my unruly hair has always re-quired an oil truck's worth of hair glue to keep in place, I could now get away with simply washing, drying, and slightly tousling my hair, a development most notoriously indicated by the phe-nomenal popularity of a Broadway musical on the subject with a one-word title that was not *Cats* or *Evita* (which came rather later). My style changes were a bit of a coming-out party without any sexual innuendo, and I think I learned to relax somewhat, as well as come across a little more forcefully than I had previ-ously dared.

One morning as I walked past the receptionist, looking straight ahead at the Statue of Liberty seemingly seated on a carpet of clouds with nothing around it visible (a breathtaking view some version of which greeted me every working day), I heard Dick call me in. Since my office was right next door to his, I dumped my coat and briefcase and bounced into one of the upholstered chairs across from him. Thinking maybe we had just gotten a new deal he wanted me to work on, I was getting pumped up, but then he assumed a serious look and his usual voice dropped at least an octave.

"Mike," he said, "there's something we need to talk about." He folded his hands and leaned forward. He had been a federal prosecutor before joining the firm, and he knew how to play the role convincingly. My blood went cold as I leaned toward him and asked, with all the newly developed forcefulness I could call upon, what that might be. "It's a very big day for you," he said, pausing, "because today is the day you decide whether you're going to become part of the mail-room staff, or go across the street into the basement and get yourself a fucking haircut, whether you think you need one or not."

It was an odd feeling. In one moment the earth had opened up to consume me, never to be seen or heard from again, and in the next we were in a Punch and Judy show, with Dick as the puppet master. But what wouldn't go away was the never-to-be-forgotten realization that I was being watched. People were discussing my behavior and appearance and would always do so, no matter how free and easy I felt. I might decide to do X, Y, or Z, based on what I gleaned, but in the future, before taking any steps, I would need to check with someone "in the know," which had never, at any of the multitudinous places I had lived in or been involved with, been me. I had forgotten to put two and two together, and left myself exposed. Bless Dick for having made the situation funny, but his humorous presentation contained an arrow pointing in the direction of conformity that was important to attend to.

In the end, that experience proved not to have been so horrible. I did tend to my knitting and watch my back, and thus was promoted and rewarded to a satisfying degree. A side benefit was the arrival of a new, and newly single, female attorney and the arrival of love in the first degree at our annual Christmas party, at which the entertainment was a friend of the office manager who had a portable keyboard and, as I recall, could only play "Proud Mary," although that cannot possibly have been true. Our romance flamed, the matter was discussed in the partnership, and (as in all law firm decisions) a conclusion was reached based purely on the economics. A star student in the classes of a partner who had just spent a sabbatical teaching at a very good law school, she was already highly productive as one of our associate lawyers, so, all other issues aside, she could stay. Our marriage was allowed to flower into ripeness.

Dick was a popular partner. He had no airs and was simplicity itself, in an adequately complicated way. Plus, he frequently invited associate lawyers to the lunch club the firm subsidized, and he was a good teacher with a sense of humor. I learned that again in due time. My wife had just found out she was pregnant, and had worked late into the night on a deal with Dick, a public offering at the financial printer's establishment. The deal was done, as was her part, but well on the late side, so she pleaded fatigue and Dick gave her the day off.

As I left for work that morning, a tile man Dick had recommended to us when we admired the work on his terrace arrived to lay down some terra-cotta tile in the apartment we had just bought, which was of late '20s vintage and had a stunning view of Central Park and the Museum of Natural History. However, it contained blue-and-yellow-patterned linoleum in the kitchen and pantry that dated from the building's opening. The tile man's assistant inadvertently let ash from his cigarette fall into a five-gallon can of mastic (adhesive to bond the tile to the cement floor). The can went off like napalm, torching the entire back half of our apartment, and my wife dashed through the flames out the service entrance, finding refuge with a neighbor upstairs and calling me, within a minute of the time I sat down at my desk, to tell me the story.

The rest of the day was consumed with coping with the disaster. The fire had been hot enough to melt the gold rims on our china inside the sturdy wooden cabinets in the kitchen, so that the plates were now joined together, drips of gold linking each plate to the one underneath. When I later saw a can of mastic, the warnings were in red, and four times as long as the instructions for use. During the ensuing litigation, we learned about a case in which a workman was using it in a Long Island frame house, and the vapor exuding from the open can found its way to the pilot light on the clothes dryer in the next room, ignited, and blew the man through the side of the house!

The next morning, on my way into my office, I stopped at Dick's door and thanked him for his recommendation of the tile layer, pausing to dwell at some length on the previous day's disaster and the new pregnancy's involvement therein. He put down his coffee, got up from behind his desk, and shook my hand vigorously, saying with enthusiasm, "She's pregnant! That's wonderful. Listen, I know a great obstetrician!"

So, in this case, the question of siblings we began with may have a simple answer or none at all. With their father's status as a Manhattan federal judge, Reginald A, six years older than Dick, was clearly assigned the responsibility of holding up the family reputation and carrying forth the legacy of substantial achievement. He managed to do it so thoroughly that Dick, having the type of freer temperament that is often the benefit of being a younger sibling, as well as a lively brain and considerable self-possession, concluded that he was off the hook—though not so far off that he didn't put time in on government service and then become a partner in a first-class law firm.

The punch line, so to speak, is that his daughter went to Harvard and ended up as the head writer on *Sex in the City*. One might say that he had learned the lesson he later taught me, that marching to the sound of your own drummer is fine, as long as that drummer is enough like the drummer the rest of the clan feels at home with.

XV SAME OLD SAME OLD?

ONE OF THE MOST intimate ways in which the small-world truism applies occurs when you meet someone who shares your name, which has happened to me twice in a fairly long lifetime.

A bar named O'Lunney's on 2nd Avenue near 48th Street in Manhattan, near the UN, had live music every Friday and Saturday and a decent-sized dance floor. The atmosphere was energetic and cheerful—a lot of young ladies from abroad and many from the City as well were to be found there, and the band played a kind of Texas Tornadoes song list, with some Motown thrown in, all of which was easy to dance to. In short, it was a Happy Hunting Ground in the best sense of the phrase, and I spent many glad nights there over several years.

Most of the time the band was headed by Alger Mitchell, a good-looking, typical front-man guitar player, tall and cowboy lean. Brian Slawson, the drummer, had been nominated for a Grammy based on his solo version of "The Well-Tempered Clavier" played on wood blocks with felt-covered hammers and entitled "Bach on Wood." But the point of this story is the keyboard man, an even-tempered young guy who played piano and synthesizer and had the same name as me except for having a double R in his last name where I make do with a single—which, coincidentally, is wise advice for long sojourns in a bar like that.

I was there often enough to get friendly with the band, young, cheerful, and optimistic except for the bass player, who was from a generation closer to mine and always hung out on the periphery when the band took five and headed out for a smoke of whatever and a beer. Over time I bought beers for them and did some small-time folding-money tipping. A halfway thoughtful guy will soon recognize this as the way to a band's heart, which connects with many a girl's heart because during the breaks there were always more girls than could be counted, which meant more than there would be band members, and with me being an unofficial mascot who might be taken for their manager if you didn't follow up your surmise with a confirmational question, it was ground zero for opportunity.

A serious NYC groupie during the Golden Age of the Fillmore East, Max's Kansas City, CBGB, and the like told me that the well-established groupie hierarchy worked out so that the drummer always got last pick, after the other band members had made their selections. Brian was actually the member I had the most interesting conversations with. I had never paid much attention to anything but lyrics and guitar riffs, while he knew a lot about music and liked to expound. Also, being with Brian meant that I was now the default low man on the totem pole, if you know which pole I mean.

Brian later got a job lasting several years with the road company of *Hair* or *Cats* (if you think about it, *Cats* was *Hair* but with fur). I got a postcard of the Washington Monument from him that mentioned his having smoked crack with Mayor Berry, but after that we lost touch. Michael Parrish disappeared one August when the city was shut down, and when I asked about him everyone said he'd gone down to Nashville to try his hand as a studio musician there.

About a decade later I had settled down, bought a co-op, and taken up golf. Playing golf was kind of expected at my workplace, and was a good way to do business on Wall Street, which had become my fate. My game not being all that good, I tried to get in some practice at Van Cortlandt Park in the Bronx near the Yonkers city line, one of the two oldest public courses in the country, and not a bad taxi ride when fares still stopped below fifteen dollars instead of starting there. It was also accessible by subway, so I decided to try that and made a tee time over the phone, because I did not and still do not trust machines to look after me honestly and accurately. Most of us know that nowadays but refuse to admit it. I still call and talk to a person before I ever go out to play, which has held confusion and error to virtually nil.

But on the first ride out, which I saved for a weekday I was able to play hooky on, I discovered that most of the way was local stops—several hundred of them, it felt like—and then a good twenty-minute hike, toting my clubs, to the pro shop. Not surprisingly, I missed my tee time by a good half hour, but the starter told me he'd get me on the course pretty soon, so I should just hang around and pretend to be looking for a new golf shirt or buying some balls until I heard my name called.

In about ten minutes that happy event took place. At the same time I said yes, so did a younger man, wearing jeans cut off below the knee, a yellow Hawaiian shirt, and a Panama hat, on the other side of the starter's desk. He had a very light bag with him, not outside on the bag rack, and his clubs were all actual wooden-variety woods, an ensemble of irons of various vintages, and a putter I recognized as the same kind my dad had used—not to much effect—when I'd caddied for him in junior high many years earlier. So we were to play together, two Mike Par(r)ishes, and were both young enough to walk the course. After we paid and were walking to the first tee, I told him about our mutual namesakeness and a little about O'Lunney's and my having lost track of that Mike when he went off to Nashville. He stopped dead, flexed his knees, and put out his arms in a bear-hug stance, saying with a manly giggle, "It's me, baby! I'm back!"

It was great. He hadn't changed much at all, so to meet my namesake again after all that time was a hoot and set a wonderful tone for our round of golf, which involved two par fives, almost seven hundred yards long, built for Babe Ruth when he was with the Yankees. Most perfect of all, his game was no better than mine despite his age advantage. Afterward, he gave me a ride back to the Upper West Side, where (naturally enough) we both had taken root, first digging around in the back of his Ford Fairlane wagon among a cornucopia of paraphernalia to favor me with a copy of his one recording so far. *Automobility* was selling modestly but continually, and he would be going back to Nashville once he finished a couple more songs for the next one. I looked at the CD, thanked him, and laughed out loud on our way out of the Bronx and into what passes in New York City for civilization when I saw that the lead song was one I remember him playing with the band at O'Lunney's—"Psychedelic Cowboy, Rasta Muslim, Working on His PhD/Studyin' Appalachian Strummin', African Drummin' and Tantric Musicology." We shared a warm good-bye outside my co-op building and I never saw him again. You know a happy ending when you run smack dab into one like we did, and you let it be.

———

Sometime after that I returned for the fortieth anniversary celebration of the founding of my high school, McLean High in Fairfax County, northern Virginia. When we moved to the area, my father was finishing thirty years in the U.S. Army. He started by training infantry troops for the Pacific Theater, then led a rifle company in hand-to-hand combat in the Philippines and MacArthur's island campaign. After that we spent seven years in Germany as he tracked down Nazis in hiding, physically and identity-wise, with some other stops. Virginia was the first place I ever lived more than eighteen months, and McLean was the only high school other than Fairfax High, in the town that was the county capital. Now there are about a dozen high schools.

McLean then was mostly farmland, plus split-level and ranch-style single-family developments just starting to erupt like teenage acne or worse, if that's possible. Along the Potomac sat high-end manor houses, some of which dated back before the Civil War, and others built for river views offered from the flat-roofed International- or Bauhaus-style new residences. While there, I raked leaves and split logs for dating money on the well-forested property of Stuart Udall, JFK's secretary of the interior, from the famous Western family of conservationists and political figures—probably the first modern mansion set deep in the woods that I had ever encountered.

McLean High's territory on the more southerly side was an area known as Pimmit Hills that dated from the previous century. Working-class and artisan families had been there for decades, and were typically blue-collar and classically Southern. In the beginning, while the housing developments started springing up closer to the Potomac, that stock provided the school with three or four very successful years of football, basketball, and baseball teams which led to championships, plus several pro athletes. Some of them had classic, Faulknerian names like Cline Mutersbaugh, Cantwell Muckenfuss, and Reid Thrasher, but over time those teams became more mediocre, while the chess team I was on won the Northern Virginia championship. Of the top ten kids in my class, eight became full professors at prestigious universities, one is in charge of the Holocaust section at the National Archives, and then there was me, with two Ivy degrees and not a molecule of scholarly temperament in the whole of my body or brain.

McLean rapidly became the CIA high school as nearby Langley saw the new headquarters coming into existence there. A few students went off to boarding school, but there was an upper crust of kids whose families lived nearer the river or in a few developments dating from shortly after the Depression, when the government started morphing toward its present form. Our most famous grad was Richard (Ricky) Ames, the CIA traitor in later life who was responsible for the deaths of numerous undercover agents in the U.S.S.R., whose father was a senior officer at "The Company," mother was chair of our English department, and older sister was head cheerleader and homecoming queen. I dated a girl in my class whose dad was one of the highest-up people in the agency and, since this is a story of namesakes, I can sneak in the story of how she got her own name. She arrived back from Germany halfway through our junior year. Her dad had been in the OSS during World War II—the "Wild Bill" Donovan days before Allen Dulles was commissioned to turn that into the CIA.

She was born in 1943 on November 11, the height of the war and patriotic fever, and her dad was in uniform but stateside. As a hyper-traditionalist and very devoted to her lovely and elegant mother, he declared, for reasons apparently based on the fact that she would be the only natural child they would ever have, that her name should be the same as her mother's, but with the word "Junior" appended to it.

Her parents were unable to settle this disagreement, until two days after the birth, when her father came to her mother's hospital room and said he was on his way to the maternity office in the hospital to sign the certificate and specify the name. In those days, new mothers were confined to bed for a week or more and had no mobility whatsoever outside of their rooms. He knew he had her between a rock and a hard place, which he made clear by saying that if she didn't agree to his wishes, this only daughter would be certified, christened, and known for the rest of her life as "Armisticia," in honor of her birth, and of the thousands of Americans who had died in World Wars I and II, and had died and would die in the one still far from conclusion and uncertain in its result.

So she agreed, and that was that. But in the end, it worked out all right and the Junior never proved to be a problem. Many girls share their mother's name, so everyone assumed that pendant abbreviation was some kind of typo or scrivener's error, and ultimately it went the way of the hoop skirt and button shoes.

In our era, the kids on their way to institutions of higher learning all followed the dress code and haircuts of the Ivy League and the Seven Sisters women's colleges plus Sweetbriar, Newton College of the Sacred Heart, Rosemont, and other properly named places for proper young ladies. We wore button-down shirts and khakis, although some of the khakis had buckles in the back between the beltline and the pockets, some adjustable and some just for show, and were called "Heinie Binders." Future geeks and dweebs also wore plastic pocket protectors to hold the multicolored pens they would use in math and science classes. The guys who were about to conclude their formal educations wore "bomber" loafers with exaggeratedly thick black soles, or cowboy boots or work boots like construction laborers sport, and pegged pants, which were tight fitting and became narrower as they reached the shoe tops. They also used a ton of hair oil and grease and combed their hair back along the sides and with a curl like Elvis had, arching down past the middle of their foreheads, and a "DA," or duck's ass, jointure at the back.

The fortieth reunion was held at a Four Seasons hotel in Tysons Corner, now a large mid-rise complex of Pentagon and military contractors, consultants, and computer specialists, with a shopping center consisting of the likes of Nordstrom, Saks, Needless Markup (as we called it), and the Mark Crosses, Cross Pens, and Gucci Gulch loafer purveyors who greatly postdated our era. Nearby you could find the first elite Giant Food Store, a big chain in the DC area, whose gourmet and imported food sections had become larger than those of the "normal" grocery store.

In our day, Route 123, aka Chain Bridge Road (to the Potomac and DC), was a two-lane highway obviously built by military engineers, as evidenced by its undeviating straightness. There was a TV antenna for a local, non-network station and a one-story cinder block building where you could bring your cattle or the deer and game birds you had shot to be butchered, individually wrapped, and stowed in the twelve-foot horizontal freezers many families kept in their garages. We also knew very well about the straightness of the highway because both Chain Bridge and similarly designed and constructed Georgetown Pike (from DC up to Great Falls farther north and also quite undeveloped) were designed, many years previously, to expedite military traffic in general but especially—if you can imagine this—to promptly repel invasions.

So what we did on weekends was go on double dates to athletic events, followed by sock hops in the gyms, then find places to park for an hour or two along gravel roads leading to utility substations back in the high brush, drop the girls at one or both of their homes, and finally head out for Chain Bridge or Georgetown Pike to see if my dad's Bel Air Chevy with its V-8 engine, once the largest-selling car in U.S. history, could break 100 miles per hour, and mostly it could. It took two to pull this off, one to hold the wheel steady and push the gas pedal, and the other to watch the speedometer and shout when the deed was done, since, as dumb as we were, we knew better than to try that all on our own.

Going into the reunion dinner, it was refreshing not only to see a few recognizable faces, but also to observe that the DAs (even if gray or graying), pegged pants, and sport coats with two vents in the back had held their own, as had their dates' fancy hairdos that still owed more to Scarlett O'Hara than to *Vogue*. Turtlenecks, possibly turtleneck tops without bodies or sleeves, abounded in certain segments of the alumni body. We were seated at tables organized in five-year segments. The school had been set up with varsity sports reserved for grades 10–12 and the 7th and 8th graders in a separate part of the facility. This permitted me to meet my other namesake, as he came and stood behind the empty chair next to me and asked if someone was sitting there, permitting me to give my stock answer of "You are," which always gets a smile and establishes a warmth that almost never fails to set a good tone.

I stood up and we shook hands. Then we looked at our name tags and chuckled. He was actually five years younger, so we had never shared any space, much less classes or sports. He pointed a finger at me and said, "Your phone number was Elmwood 6-4454" as we sat down. I laughed and nodded, then asked him why he would know and remember a thing like that.

It was simple, he told me. His father's name was John, just like my dad's, and unlike my keyboard-playing namesake, his family also did without the second R in Par(r)ish. But his father's middle initial was C, for Charles, while mine was M, for Mitchell, and thus their listing was earlier in the phone directory. Since my father was an Army lifer who had many friends and acquaintances having business with the Defense Department and many other government agencies and entities, the John Cs would get five or six calls a week, always after ten-thirty at night, placed by one or more of those friends from bars or officers' or NCO clubs that were closing very soon, and who had been more interested in addressing that dimension of their evening they were about to conclude than remembering to arrange for somewhere to sleep, like a room at a BOQ (Bachelor Officers' Quarters) at one of the numerous military establishments in and around Washington.

His father quickly tired of the late-night calls (for school-aged kids and probably for parents in those days before Jack Paar and Steve Allen created the late-night talk show on TV). He had gotten my family's phone number and taped up a piece of paper next to the phone—almost no one had two phones then—bearing these words: "Do you have a pen or pencil and something to write on? PAUSE. OK. The number you want is Elmwood 6-4454. Let me repeat that. REPEAT. OK. Good luck and please don't call again. That's all you need. Good luck and good night."

That message was so well-designed and the information (in those days before area codes) so succinct that no one ever called back, just as I have never seen or heard from that Mike Parish again. Still, I was glad to learn a little bit more about my family and the incredibly separate, secret life my father led, since I was never awake when the calls came in. We actually had two phones, one paid for by the military and in my parents' bedroom, since my father's security clearance was "COSMIC TOP SECRET" and his job was catching Russian spies, so he always had to be on call.

XVI SHE LAUGHED

EVERY BLOCK around Central Park has its catalogue of the rich, famous, and powerful. Ours had Mr. Spock, aka Leonard Nimoy, and across the way Margaret Mead in her turret at the Museum of Natural History, plus two future publishers of the *New York Times*, father and then-eight-year-old son, and the guy who wrote both "Coke Is It," *and* "Join the Pepsi Generation," together with the leading stock analyst of his generation in the realm of Big Pharma (before it was known by that sobriquet), who shall remain nameless in case the statute of limitations hasn't expired in all jurisdictions. Let us say that he was never an insider, so more likely than not he was simply prescient but never corrupt (and his identity will be confined herein to the information that his mother, after divorcing his father, lived over and often frequented the Cedar Bar, which during its heyday was the watering hole of Pollack, Larry Rivers, Rauschenberg, Johns, Morris Louis or Louis Morris—whatever his name was—Baselitz, and de Kooning, and his second-earliest memories involve them pounding on his mother's front door well after midnight with their shoes and howling her name and nicknames, now long interred with their genius). Erica Jong (*Fear of Flying* and its legendary zipless fuck) lived two doors down, and my daughter's best friend's father was an eighth-generation Harvard alum who worked for the Rockefellers and whose family owned the piece of turf where the Battle of Concord (By the rude bridge that arched the flood, / blah blah blah blah blah

blah / Here once the embattled farmers stood / And fired the shot heard round the world) was fought *when* it was fought. We also featured the cellist in the world's greatest string quartet at that time. But mostly we were the block where they blew up the balloons for what N'Yorkers call "The Macy's Day Parade," and you could hear the bullhorns call out at three in the morning, "More helium for Woody Woodpecker, please, on the double."

Despite all the surrounding celebrity, the kids in our building were subject to the usual formless fears and baseless torments, plus a few real ones not known or discussed otherwise than *en famille*. In my daughter's case, my first experience with being regarded as the greatest dad in the world arose when she was just four and came into our bedroom at 4 a.m. screaming that bees were attacking her eyes and they wouldn't go away. She was holding her hands over them as she cried, and I told her to open them. Ipso facto, the bees went away, and she hugged me for all she was worth, telling me I had saved her, and more along that line, then came to bed between us, awaking with a version of the same smile that had greeted the disappearance of the bees. Later, HBO showed up, bringing us *Gallipoli* with Mel Gibson rushing into Turkish machine-gunfire never to be seen again, while she was lying between us late in her fifth year, and we were nearly condemned to death for allowing her to watch that agonizing, heartbreaking scene of the useless, insane deaths of an entire regiment of Aussie soldiers due to Winston Churchill's ambition. We felt even guiltier than Churchill must have felt at the time, which now evokes a wish that we and she had been gifted with the knowledge of what a scoundrel Gibson became as his actual self in the not-too-distant future.

But the jewel in the crown of our place of residence was someone no one has ever heard of (no one I know or have met, at least), but whom I became privileged to know, one way and another. His name was Ralph Shikes, and he and his wife, Ruth, lived in the penthouse above us in a building that was a hollow square, abutting the New York Historical Society standing on the corner of 77th and Central Park West, with the C-shaped three quarters of the square on the east adjacent to the museum and the I-shaped, most westerly part accessed by another door, thereby closing the square. When we had our obligatory fire while remodeling the kitchen, before my daughter was born, my wife skibbled (as she termed it) through the flames and ran upstairs three flights to find refuge with the Shikeses, who were significantly older (we were quite young for our ages!), and infinitely more gracious and accommodating, so we became friends by virtue of having been burned out on their watch and thus invited to the book party Ralph's publisher threw for him at their apartment when his majestic catalogue raisonné of Pissarro—in many ways the father of the Impressionist movement—was published.

Ralph was old Harvard at its best. Where the money came from never arose in conversation, nor need it have. He could remember from his early teens seeing the Hoovervilles established on the north side of Central Park South behind the wall and twenty-foot drop to the soil. When he majored in art in college, one of the first things he did was collect, and then put out, a book of black-and-white engravings, drawings, and prints by radical artists, politically engaged geniuses like Hogarth, Daumier, Goya, Kollwitz, Max Beckmann, and Otto Dix called *The Indignant Eye*, which was his eye engaged with the injustice, cruelty, and hypocrisy that fueled most of the wars of the last several centuries, if not all before as well. That book was both the forerunner and the standard against which all the future work in this realm was regarded and measured.

In the midst of his research and assemblage of the material necessary for his Pissarro book, Ralph learned—because he was nothing if not in the loop as to these issues—that the painter's heirs had decided they were short of money, since so few paintings had come down to them in the course of time. Pissarro was a hard-core left-wing socialist who managed not only to gather around him in a suburb not far from Paris a group of phenomenal artistic talents whose sympathies lay not with their clients but with the humble subjects of their work, but also to produce the work necessary to fund the gathering and rearing of a good-sized family while he was at his social mission. It was not by accident that Ralph had homed in on Camille Pissarro as his pole star and ego ideal.

The conclusion of those heirs, two or three generations removed from their wellspring, was to gather together all of the letters their own forebears received from the artist and have them auctioned off in a small number of lots, not too many and not too few, carefully constructed like one of his masterworks, so that the essence of his thought was parceled across those lots with an effort at equivalence of value as well as the expansion thereof.

Ralph flew to Paris and bought them all, his manifest determination most probably shoving aside other bidders—dealers, connoisseurs, speculators—so that the letters could be combined with those already archived institutionally and preserved for scholars and the public at large, including Ralph's own work, to the extent he would draw on and incorporate them in his analysis and depiction.

The year after Ralph's book came out, I was walking my daughter back from a birthday party on the west side of Columbus Avenue onto our home block. She had a bag of goodies, of course, which I was carrying, of course, and in the hand that was not held in mine, she had a yellow balloon filled with helium. As we got about five or six steps onto our side of the avenue, the balloon popped with a noise loud enough to be heard, despite the buses and other constant traffic. (When she first went off to summer camp, she wrote us that it was hard to get to sleep at night because of the absence of cabs honking and the sirens of police, ambulances, and firemen, not to mention the subterranean roar of the A train in the midst of its enormous voyage from 59th to 125th, the longest subway run in all of New York City.)

I did the natural thing, which was to drop down on my knees and hug her, comfort her for her loss, and hold her tight to keep her from crying. At just that moment I heard Ralph's voice, less than ten feet away, calling my name sharply. As I wrapped my arms around her, I looked back at him. He was pointing upward—at the past, in a sense—at the long-gone balloon, shouting to me, "Mike! She laughed! She laughed!" Which was the only thing we really needed to know.

XVII A LOSER IS A LOSER

THREE THINGS that have been linked in New York City forever are sports, betting, and crime. Now that the Supreme Court has permitted legalized gambling in New Jersey, New York won't be far behind, even though its Off-Track Betting experiment failed, possibly because it was operated by the government. The greatest American novel set in New York bears the fictionalized name of the New York mobster who fixed the 1919 World Series, and every bar in the City worth its name has a football pool and is full of patrons who know the spreads and the over and under on every NFL game every week, and for the NBA three times weekly. When Jack Molinas, a Columbia grad with a genius for fixing college basketball games in the early '60s at The Garden, was later killed in his Hollywood Hills backyard by an expert marksman using a scope sight, the headline being "Only Question With Molinas Killing Is Which Mob," he was still identified in the first line of the story as a New Yorker.

This came into focus for me late one summer in the '90s at Shea Stadium. I shared season tickets for the Mets with seven friends for a few years. Each spring we would meet in a conference room at Teachers Insurance on Lexington in the 40s and do a round-robin draw of the eighty-two home games, with the first two going to the organizer for his efforts, and again in the fall—the Mets were good in some of those years—for playoff and World Series tickets. I got to see a game they lost 1–0 to the Braves when Mike Piazza threw over the second baseman's head on a steal attempt and the base runner came around to score the game's only run!

The situation in question was unusual since I had exchanged my regular ticket because of a work conflict, and ended up attending a day game on a Wednesday I somehow had free. Because of the exchange, I landed in the upper deck slightly to the left field side of home plate, but with good visibility. The Padres were our opponent, and the game was lightly attended—we played them only two series a year, and there was no rivalry to speak of. They were the one West Coast team with no New York connection, were almost always in the lower depths of the standings, and their games in California were televised when all of us were asleep or otherwise occupied.

The big attraction, if there was one, was great weather and the presence of Anthony Young on the mound for us. If he lost again today, it would be twenty-six losses in a row, a new major league record. From what I could tell, most fans were hoping he could "get off the schneid," as the saying goes, but the guy in the seat one over from me was almost foaming at the mouth in his enthusiasm for Young to take another fall and set the new ignominious record.

He was an athletic-looking guy in his late twenties, dressed in tennis whites and matching shoes with about a pound and a half of gold jewelry on his wrists and shining out through his red, curly, and super-abundant chest hair, matched by a sort of Izro (Israeli Afro) haircut and a further abundance on his arms and legs. If you had to guess what his name might be, you might say Furry Murray (got a new kind of haircut, now Murray ain't furry anymore, the song says). The only natural redheads in our species are Russian Jews and people of Celtic descent, but the Russians are curlier by far. If man buns had been in then, he would have been a poster boy for the look.

When the first Padre up singled, my neighbor almost turned inside out with joy, but Young quickly settled down and retired the next twenty-three batters. The guy beside me remained animated the whole time, berating Young and vociferously pulling for the Pods' hitters, but to little effect. Several times I asked him why he was so hard on Young, and he kept repeating, "A loser is a loser, that's all." The game slogged on, and my clearest memory is of the most flavorful bratwurst I ever had anywhere. Upper deck, few fans, and the warm day collaborated to slowly dry the wurst out on the grill and concentrate the taste immeasurably, almost to the point of caramelization. The game was scoreless at the end of seven.

I was still enjoying the memory of the wurst when the top of the eighth rolled around and the second batter got on base with a walk. My neighbor immediately became agitated, shouting, "No time like now" and his mantra, "A loser is a loser." The next batter was Archi Cianfrocco, right-hand-hitting third baseman—low-average hitter but with some power.

At this point it becomes important to switch the focus to the Mets' right fielder, Bobby Bonilla, New York born and recently acquired from the Pirates. A regular All-Star when in the Pirate outfield with Barry Bonds, Bonilla got a rich contract from the Mets but never performed up to that same level again. Many said he had too many fast friends of all sorts in his hometown to keep his mind on baseball. Bonilla later played on the Florida Marlins when they bested the Yankees in the '03 World Series, but he ultimately wore out his welcome everywhere he played with poor performance and endless complaints about playing time.

Several pitches into the at-bat, Cianfrocco launched a high fly ball to the opposite field and the crowd rose to its feet. From where I stood, I had a perfect line on the ball and followed it as it descended and Bonilla leapt to try to snag it. He rose up just as the ball came down and I could clearly see the ball descend, right between his outstretched glove and his Mets cap, missing each by about eight inches, like a field goal settling down between the uprights for a score.

Cianfrocco received his congratulations at home plate and

on re-entering the dugout, and Anthony Young kicked the dirt next to the rubber. A Little Leaguer could have made that catch with no trouble, but Bonilla found a way, against all odds, to make Anthony Young a piece of baseball history. Young died of a brain tumor at fifty-one in 2017. My good neighbor was leaping up and down like he was at an Orthodox wedding doing the Kazotsky. I even succumbed to high-fiving him, and finally we sat down. After a moment he leaned over to me and smiled, saying, "Bobby Bo just made me twenty-five K, my friend. I got ten-to-one odds on Young breaking the record. A loser is a loser. Don't ever forget it! Here's to me."

The footnote that brings the story full circle is that Bonilla later came back to the Mets, still under the grossly overpaid contract he'd gotten in the first place. The Mets at that point would have had to pay him $6.8 million to terminate the contract, but Fred Wilpon, the Mets' owner, was heavily invested with Bernie Madoff, possibly the most famous criminal in the history of American finance, who was paying out a steady 10 percent to his original investors, using money he was taking in from new ones lured by his phony returns. The interest on the Bonilla contract settlement was 8 percent, so Wilpon put the money with Madoff and laughed all the way home over the 2 percent spread he would be reaping by deferring his payments until the period 2009 to 2035. So now Bonilla, without playing a single game, gets $1.19 million every year in July on what is informally celebrated as "Bobby Bo Day," and Fred Wilpon, finally understanding that the joke was on him, holds Bernie Madoff's IOU.

So if you want to know what went wrong with the New York Mets, ask yourself this. How can Fred Wilpon, an accountant by training, make a decision based on the following assumptions? He puts about $6 million with Bernie Madoff in 1993 and gets 10 percent a year on it every year, without fail, until 2035 or later. Which is to say he makes simple interest of 420 percent, not even compounded interest on that amount, and during that period the one thing he can be sure of is that the $6 million is accruing

8 percent annual interest. With Bernie Madoff, who also shoots 83 every time he goes out on the golf course, without fail. What's wrong with the New York Mets? Is a loser a loser, or what? Am I right, or am I right?

———

Fifteen years later, I was reminded of that game and Bonilla's goof when I went to Rikers Island for the first and only time. Janos, a high school buddy of my son's, was at Fordham Law School. As a public service project, he had organized a "moot court" on Sundays in the juvenile section for teenagers who qualified for more contact with the outside world. Aside from what we don't know about a ton of countries we support with aid and arms and probably torture techniques, Rikers is the largest prison on the planet, and people wait there, sometimes for years, to go to trial. As noted earlier, New York and crime are said in the same breath almost as often as not.

A moot court is a mock trial, and forms part of every law school education. Two law students play the attorneys for the plaintiff and defendant, and others are witnesses, jury members, or court officers—almost like on Judge Judy and Judge Wapner of *Rain Man*, but they do only civil cases, where one citizen sues another. There is also a set of facts based on something like the arresting officer's report; we did only criminal cases at Rikers. Janos sent the fact sheet over during the week and the officers distributed it, then helped the inmates decide who would play what role. We visitors, some lawyers and some law students, were the judges and coached the lawyers.

Once the trials got under way, it was fascinating to see how difficult it was for the prosecutors to put together a case and present it in an orderly way, while the defense teams were very sharp and aggressive. You could see this was the side they had studied and learned about from their experience. The six trials were held in the gym, using that kind of geometrical Naugahyde stuffed red, yellow, and blue furniture that can be arranged in different ways for group activities. My judicial bench reached just above my knees, and I sat on a cubical ottoman about the height of the bench, but once we got started everyone played it straight.

This week's case involved the arrest of a young man living in a project who had been arrested for sticking up a bodega, taking money and a pack of cigarettes, then being found later with twelve of the cigarettes but without the original pack. Those wise to the ways of the ghetto know that cigarettes are normally sold there in parcels of three, which I learned during the trial. Given the participants, Janos told me beforehand, very few guilty verdicts were returned.

Before we reached the first witness, we had to undergo the normal screening, which took more than half an hour. Then we were marched down to the gym and watched for another half hour as the boys, and then the furniture, were added to the scene and the "courtrooms" were set up. All of this time provided leisure to inspect the surroundings, which generally looked like any other junior high or high school basketball court you've ever seen, including two sets of fold-up, wooden bleachers on either side.

What I noticed was that the wall above the west basket was painted with the jerseys of ten NBA greats. Walt "Clyde" Frazier was there to represent the Knicks, partly due to his still doing live commentary for the games on TV. Clyde may have said "The Knicks are playing defense with their hands and not with their feet" a few times too often for my taste, but he was never wrong when he said it. Then, too, one of my best early memories of NYC was riding in a cab uptown through the narrow tunnel on Park Avenue around 33rd to 37th Streets and seeing the smiling face of a man driving a Rolls Royce and wearing a white mink coat and matching fedora behind the wheel of a car with the license plate "WCF" on his way to work.

The other jerseys featured an interesting mix of young and

old heroes, black and white—Jordan, Bird, Dr. J, Maravich, Kareem, Shaq, Russell, Wilt Chamberlain, and Cousy. A surprise to me was Rasheed Wallace, a tough and combative black forward of recent vintage who in many ways exemplified an ego ideal for the young men who saw these precincts the most often. Then there was one jersey that had been painted over in a medium-blue, not too dark, that allowed you to see, when you looked closely, whose name it bore. Isiah Thomas—Isiah Lord Thomas III on his birth certificate. NBA Hall of Famer, two-time NBA champion, twelve-time NBA All-Star, NCAA champion with an undefeated Bobby Knight Indiana team, Olympic gold medal winner, leader of the "bad boy" Detroit Pistons, married man, and by most accounts an all-around creep and low-life scumbag.

When the lamentable Knicks owner James Dolan made him president of the club, Thomas ended up costing the team $11.6 million for sexual harassment of a woman who had a strong résumé at a high level in women's basketball. Then Dolan, to universal opprobrium, hired him back. Thomas has hung around basketball despite having become a pariah, and presumably has nothing else to do. What resonated with me was that here in this criminal establishment, the street-wise adolescents to whom NBA basketball is most likely greater than religion—the dream of every black kid in America—the collective insight of the inmates was clear. He didn't belong on any wall of heroes. His memory deserved to be extinguished. I have said for many years that I learned more from my two children than I ever did from my parents, and if there's anyone out there who has ever seen a college athlete say "Hi Dad" when the camera crew approaches him on the sideline, I'd like to see the evidence. Mom comes first, always. We have learned a lot more than we wanted to know about the Isiah Thomases of the world in recent times, but we are much better off for it, better off by far.

XVIII NYC DOWNTOWN LAWYERS' SOFTBALL LEAGUE

BEFORE I HEAD OUT to the USS *Hornet* on San Francisco Bay for tonight's New Year's Eve celebration, freezing my butt off and watching the SF fireworks, I have to write this, speaking as "Scoops," which became my official team name in the NYC Downtown Lawyers' Softball League, after I made the transition many veteran catchers necessarily make to playing first base.

I got the name the night we were playing Breed, Abbott in the best-played softball game I've ever seen or been in, and not just because I drove in the winning run—indeed, the sole run—in a 1–0 victory. In part, it's also because when our opponents had a guy on second in the bottom of the last inning and two out, the hitter bounced one to the left side. I think Mike Joye was playing third, and he heaved a brick my way, which landed in the dirt right next to the base. Mickey, our semi-pro umpire who loved the excitement of umping twilight games along the FDR on the Lower East Side compared to what he did in the daytime, was umping, and it had gotten quite dark. I dug out Mike's throw and pulled my glove toward the sky with a flourish (the guy was safe, barely), then looked at Mickey. He couldn't resist playing a role in the drama, and threw his thumb in the air.

To emphasize the finality of the call, I bounced the ball hard on the ground like I'd seen Pete Rose do with the Phillies, when they won the World Series, caught it on the way down, and rushed the mound to congratulate our pitcher for probably the only shutout in the history of that slow-pitch league. The teams mingled in mutual congratulations about what a great game it had been, except for the runner, that is. Sooner or later, I'm sure, he got over it and accepted his place in history, too. One could easily argue that, if the runner had tried to score and tie the game, I would have nailed him. Unquestionably.

The field on the north side of the Manhattan Bridge there at Houston Street also features in my own near-death experience as a young lawyer, against White & Case, who represented U.S. Steel and beat Harry Truman when he put patriotism ahead of profit during the Korean War by nationalizing the steel industry because they put commercial, high-paying customers ahead of war materiel and the Supreme Court sided, as so often, with the money.

A select few will recall that White & Case didn't have a team in the basketball league, so I had recruited a guy two years behind me at Princeton, who played center on the freshman team that included Larry Lucchino, president of the Red Sox when they broke the curse of Babe Ruth and won the World Series. Dave Blair, aka The Goon, whose wife, a Vassar girl, went by Queenie, was that guy. He had a friend, Richie Peters, at their firm who had played JV basketball at St. John's or Manhattan College and was a very smooth point guard, while The Goon was six foot four and built for power, if not for speed. They were great teammates, and we did very well with them included.

But they did have a softball team and so, one evening, there we were across the diamond from each other.

At the time, Adrian Leiby, our senior partner and my mentor, had decided to take his first vacation in thirty years or so to go to France. He had asked me (then living in a brownstone apartment in Cobble Hill Brooklyn, adjacent to Brooklyn Heights) to look after his house, the former parsonage of the First Reformed Church of Bergenfield, in whose cemetery he is now buried.

The home was a fieldstone house from the seventeenthth century, rough-cut in the style of that time. A stream ran by the edge of the property, and he had a fabulous rose garden. He had also gone to Ashlawn, President James Monroe's mansion down the hill from Monticello in Charlottesville, to take cuttings of a special kind of boxwood hedge that wintered well in Jersey, which he set in place around the roses.

The caretaker job came complete with his T-Bird, a big one with a phenomenal sound system, and his parking place in a garage on Water Street, two blocks away from our office. I started to come in late (which wasn't that unusual anyway!) to miss the traffic and boomed out the great R&R of the day, or classical, as I pleased. To be a good soldier, for softball games, I volunteered to bring some of our players and, in the capacious trunk, the equipment. After unloading on the access road, I would drive over to the first street parallel to the FDR and always find a good parking space, then come back and run some infield practice.

With White & Case, a lot of razzing was going back and forth on the field, involving Blair and Peters and our basketball team members, and the game was hotly contested. About the fourth inning, one of our sharper-eyed members asked about that cloud of black smoke back where I had stationed Leiby's car. I lit off like a bat from hell—a slow bat, of course, but probably as fast as I ever ran. When I got to the head of the street at Houston, it held firetrucks and squad cars galore. The city had repaved the street that day with a fresh coat of tar, and I had taken the first legal space on the downward slope before the fire hydrant that defined the end of legal parking—quite a nice feat, I had thought at the time.

So when the housing project kids managed to set the street on fire with the new tar as fuel, the flames had naturally followed the slope down from Houston. The fire department, bless them eternally, had put out the fire about a foot from that gorgeous T-Bird. The cops and fire guys had a good laugh, and I thanked them with all my heart. It couldn't have been a closer call, but the hood of the emerald-green vehicle had tar spots all over it. I nearly died. Then a police sergeant told me there was a gas station a few blocks west on Houston, where I could get a rag and soak it in gas, and that would dissolve the tar. Then I should just spray the car with water, although the gasoline would evaporate promptly in any event. I did as suggested and drove back to the game, finding with no effort a parking space very near my previous one—that tar wasn't going to burn again, so I was golden.

I came huffing and puffing back, quickly told the story, and found it was the bottom of the seventh, the game tied with two men on and two outs, and I was the next batter. Having heard my tale, our head litigator, Taylor Rastrick Briggs, showed a courtroom lawyer's kindness by saying, "So I guess it's med school for you after this, eh, Mike?" Meanwhile, the White & Case battery was conferring about whether to walk me intentionally, to set up a force at any base, or to pitch to me. I wish I could remember who was batting after me, but it must have been someone like Gil Ott or Rich Baxter down toward the tail end of the lineup. As they started to confer, Blair and Powers started the chant of "Pitch to the Stiff!! Pitch to the Stiff!" and so it was decided. I took a pitch and then hit one of my better shots ever into the left center field gap, but Richie Peters, their fleet-footed center fielder, made a fine running catch, and the game ended up tied because of darkness. A just result, in my opinion, which both Leiby and his good friend Judge Learned Hand (his real name, and one of the most famous judges of his day) would have had no trouble agreeing to.

XIX MR. O

AS THE OLD SAYING GOES, if the chairs could talk . . . One place where it's doubtless a good thing they can't is Bull & Bear, the bar at the Waldorf Astoria at the back side of the hotel, not the fancy Park Avenue entrance: low ceilings, a room that still feels filled with smoke years after the ban went into effect, the same staff that's been there for at least twenty-five years. When I did my first IPO, I ended up meeting with the independent accountant, a partner in one of the firms then known as the Big 8 (now the Big 4), whose signature I needed for the SEC filing package. He suggested the place, theretofore unknown to me, and bought me a couple of Remy Martins to cushion my journey back down to Wall Street to finish assembling all the documents around midnight.

More recently, I was in the midst, at about 5:30 in the afternoon, of a shaggy-dog story with Oscar, El Supremo among the bartenders, when a white-haired man with a florid complexion walked in. "Mr. O!" Oscar and several of the waiters exclaimed simultaneously. Mr. O gave a big wave and shook Oscar's hand. Oscar introduced us to each other and then confirmed that Mr. O wanted the usual.

"I haven't been up here in a while," he said, settling on his bar stool. "But we're back big time now. Got a new company and it looks like we'll be doing a deal to go public. Last one didn't work out so well—that's why I moved to Florida. Homestead exemption and all that, you know."

He laughed. "I got to know my mailman so well, from all the subpoenas and legal papers when they sued us, that I don't only know his kids' birthdays, I know their blood types and what they like to eat at McDonald's." He laughed again at his own joke and tagged me immediately as a lawyer. "But you have an honest face," he stated. "That's kind of disorienting. But it's worked for me, I know that for sure. You wouldn't know it to look at me, but I'm fifteen-sixteenths Sicilian, one part Irish. The O at the beginning of my name instead of the end has been worth its weight in gold!"

We discussed finance, Wall Street, the market, and the economy as we savored our refreshments. "You know," he said, "my wife and daughter are meeting me here. Out shopping, then we're going to Bobby Van's Steak House for dinner. She wants to go to law school, my daughter—you'll like her—and I'd appreciate it if you would talk to her, answer any questions she might have about the subject. Here, this one's on me. Confusion to the enemy."

His wife and daughter soon arrived, and we moved to the other side of the bar. With the daughter was a well-dressed man in his early thirties, short hair slicked back, nothing ostentatious. Mr. O informed me he was the fiancé, and we smiled at each other and shook hands. Mrs. O was to my left side, with the daughter in between us, and on my other side was the fiancé, Mark, with Mr. O holding down the right flank.

Miss O could not have been sweeter or more charming. We had a lovely discussion, she asked good questions, and it became apparent that she was easily smart enough to do the law thing, so I abandoned my usual reservations on the subject. My own daughter announced when she was about four that she would never be a lawyer. In response to my asking why, she said, "Well, you and mom are both lawyers, and you both hate your jobs. What am I supposed to think about that?" She's been like that all her life, and I'm sure it will always stand her in good stead.

As Miss O and I continued to meander through the legal maze, I kept an ear tuned to the conversation between Mr. O and Mark, yielding the following.

"So what's with your Uncle Tony?" Mr. O asked Mark. "I don't see him around lately. How's he doing?" Long pause, followed by throat clearing. "Well, there were some things that had to be taken care of, you know. He's not part of the picture now." Out of the corner of my eye I could see Mr. O squeeze Mark's elbow as he said, in the immediate past tense, "Well, he was that way, you know." About two minutes later, I made my exit, reminding myself to be grateful that I hadn't proffered my business card, and hoping the marriage would be as happy and carefree as possible, under the circumstances.

XX THE DON, THE LOBSTER, AND CFM III

WE ALL KNOW that Cameron F. MacRae III joined the firm as a partner in '75, as Jeff Johnson, a YLS classmate, has confirmed. Jeff's clear memory of this is evidenced by his also having "made partner" on the same day as Cam, January 1, 1975, when Cam joined his father, then the presiding partner, as a member of the firm. It was said that we had a one-vote system—Cam Senior was the man, and he had the vote.

During 1966, his last year in law school, Cam was named an editor of the *Yale Law Journal*. Another classmate of theirs and a partner in the firm as well, Chuck Burger, was there to witness the ennoblement. The setup was straightforward. Once the editors were chosen—a process I know nothing about, but it happened every year—the key event was for all of them to get individual offices along a row, each with a wooden door holding nine panes of frosted glass held in place by slender wooden strips. The minions apparently shared a table with individual work spaces.

Joining the *Journal* itself was simple then, although it has changed, as everything does. The top ten in grade-point average for the first semester were identified and anointed. At the end of the year, those in the top twenty-five but not among the original ten joined the forever elite. One member of my class finished eleventh and twenty-sixth and then tried writing a Note or Comment to gain admission, but his work was rejected by those who had edged him out. He later became general counsel for the National Organization for Women. *Res ipsa loquitur.*

After the elections and the office assignments had been taken care of, and the previous year's editors had decamped, the newbies moved in. Once that occurred, one door was found with an engraved calling card bearing the name "Cameron Farquhar MacRae III" squarely affixed by a thumbtack. Apropos of the proper style, it bore neither an address nor a telephone number. But the "Three Sticks," in Ivy League parlance, behind his name did more than speak volumes on his behalf.

The best previous story about a calling card relates to Austin Scott ("Scott on Trusts"), a notable Harvard Law student (and later professor) when Oliver Wendell Holmes held a chair there. Holmes had invited Scott, then in his third year, over for tea one Saturday, and asked him to bring a friend of his choosing from their class. As they walked over, Scott and his friend McNeil speculated about what majestic words the grand Holmes would greet them with. They were admitted, and placed their calling cards on the silver tray proffered by Holmes's butler, who took the tray upstairs and vanished, presumably by the back stairs so as not to interfere with the great man's entrance. As Holmes walked down the impressive staircase, they watched in awe as he came to greet them, playing with their cards in a random manner and saying, "First you shuffle and then you deal. Which is Scott and which McNeil?"

In the case at hand, the other six or seven offices—of the editor in chief, Articles editors, Notes and Comments editors, Book Review editors, et alia—were festooned within ten minutes by hand-lettered three-by-five index cards reading "Peter Farquhar Zimroth III," "Benno Farquhar Schmidt III," "Larry Farquhar Simon III," "Betsy Farquhar Levin III," et seq., which remained in place until the end of the academic year.

When Cam joined LeBoeuf, Lamb, Leiby & MacRae, Michael Iovenko (his predecessor at the NYS Banking Department as general counsel and then as a partner at LeBoeuf) and Donald J. Greene, our future senior partner, co-sponsored a welcoming luncheon at the City Midday Drug and Chemical Club (really—I have a small ashtray to prove it) in a private room on the south side of 140 Broadway. Our offices were in that building then, following the move from One Chase Manhattan Plaza next door. History and logic would suggest, although I cannot confirm it, that the Dewey firm, our later merger with whom soon led to the largest law firm bankruptcy in American history, had vacated those offices for us to move into as they left for elsewhere.

After cocktails, we were ushered into the dining room, with a large, hollow, square table arrangement and about thirty or so of the firm's members. Don's seat, with Cam next to him, defined the head of an otherwise headless table, and he sat in the middle of the south side of the square, with the windows and the light behind him. Iovenko sat on the right side, for whatever reason, and I recall all this because I sat opposite the three of them.

The headwaiter came around to take orders as the cocktail conversation continued, and when he got to Don, Don ordered a lobster salad and a steak. The reason I remember that is because the headwaiter asked, "A lobster salad, sir?" Don ramped up his voice so we could all hear him shout "Didn't I just say lobster salad? Are you hard of hearing?" The man nodded and moved on.

Cam Senior was not there, nor were the other name partners (now all retired or almost so). As we waited for our meals, the conversation grew more muted, due in part to a modest discomfort relating to the arrival among us of an ostensible heir apparent, but one who was certainly not to be that, since Don was making it clear who that heir would be.

Nothing unpleasant happened, but a quietude commenced to reign, interrupted only by the arrival among the appetizers of a certain lobster salad, and the reverberant response to its being placed where it had been ordered of "What the hell is this?" from Don. The waiter answered that it was the lobster salad he had ordered, rather than the more customary lobster cocktail appetizer. The salad was three times bigger, and dwarfed the vichyssoise, clam chowder, shrimp cocktail, littleneck clams, and other appetizers that now bedecked the table. The headwaiter confirmed what it was, which was immediately denied by the person we had all heard order it and then make a fuss about it. We waited while the salad was removed and a lobster cocktail substituted, after which came a lot of eating and not much talk. The main course followed, and orders for dessert were discreetly taken.

The subject on many minds was indeed hereditary succession and similar matters, and it fell to Jeff to raise the subject of King George III (surprise, surprise—Freud lives in all of us, and certainly on that occasion) of England. It had recently been determined that his madness was due to a condition known as porphyria, which afflicts those whose DNA contains the genome (neither of those words were common currency then, as they are now), and whose manifestation is caused by exposure to bright sunlight for extensive periods, which happens (if infrequently) in and around the London area in the summer.

Iovenko breathed new life into the stiffening conversation by relating a story about a dinner he'd attended at Rittenhouse Square in Philadelphia the previous weekend. The host had been a collector of rare and unusual objects and had a cabinet full of them—a miniature version of Sir John Soane's Museum in London, above Fleet Street and not far from Chancery Lane, where several shops have cash registers bearing individual keys for wigs and robes.

During Iovenko's dinner, the most remarkable object in the collector's possession was a smallish, somewhat calcified object that had been taken from its glass box and passed around. As it made its journey from hand to hand, the object was announced to have been attested to be Napoleon's penis. A bit of a giggle started to circulate at this point, loosening up our own luncheon party, and then the doors opened for the headwaiter, leading his crew of waiters bearing trays holding our desserts. He had reinvigorated himself from his previous humiliation and proudly shouted out, "Who has the Napoleon?"

Amid the uproar, one timid, slender hand was raised, to increasing laughter. Dear reader, that hand was mine. Let it ever be said that I know how to take one for the team! And the Napoleon was all anyone could have wanted.

XXI ANDALUSIA AND MOROCCO

WHEN I WAS A YOUNG LAWYER, because of extra work I had done to cover for a sick colleague, I received an extra week's vacation. I contrived to add it to my regular vacation between Labor Day weekend and Columbus Day, thereby getting a humungous amount of time off in one slug. To make the most of it, my then beloved and I decided to do Andalusia and Morocco, both of which should be on anyone's lifetime vacation roll of honor. Andalusia, although it's been done and redone, can never be done enough because of the majesty of the structures: the Alhambra in Granada, the mosque in Córdoba, all of Sevilla (which offers flamenco to boot), including a great modern art museum and a place where you can see the kinds of lock-and-key arrangements used on the Spanish treasure ships, which make up in elaboration and redundancy for what they lack in originality and sophistication.

The bottom line is that cannonballs and cutlasses captured those pieces of eight and melted-down gold bars that had, not that long previously, lived as hammered and drawn gold gardens of maize and phenomenal flowers, after which they encountered the rude smelters of the conquistadors. That way they could be transported back more efficiently to fuel the torture devices of the Inquisition and the Spanish Hapsburg dynasty, which ended in the drooling idiot rulers Goya had the genius to portray to perfection.

One of our best experiences was in Cádiz, along the harbor from which Columbus set sail once he got his funding. We saw a huge statue on a six-foot granite cube, shrouded in canvas and wrapped in strong cordage. The odds were it was a statue of Generalissimo Francisco Franco, now out of favor, but too expensive to dismantle and cart off. To our young and ingenuous eyes, though, it looked like nothing less than the Generalissimo-in-waiting between performances, the one whose death by Don Giovanni's rapier opens the great opera that begins in death and ends in damnation, while purporting to address nothing but love in all its exuberance and transgression.

Spain was slow, calculated, sinuous—a Habanera paced like the one in *Carmen*, architectural, imperious, and stolid as the sun at noon. Morocco was otherwise, foreign in every possible way, but perpetually mobile. Within five minutes of our debarking the ferry in Tangier, the protective filter on my camera lens had been unscrewed. Not the lens—I would have felt that—but something insignificant to me and worth a quarter (though it had cost five dollars) to one of the beggars who slid around like quicksand as we hauled our bags to the cab rank and shouted our hotel name five times to the driver. He pulled out at once, looking back at us the whole time and trying to both hear and read our lips before he swiveled to see what obstacles had failed to dodge out of the way of his vehicle.

Tangier, Fez, Meknes, Casablanca, and Marrakech, all built of stone, diluted concrete, and plaster, would nevertheless prove to resemble Matisse's painting named after the people who live in this country, exuding the sense that to reorder or eradicate the structures would not take much more effort than that of a fine brush held in a strong hand. It was as if the atoms interwoven to bring them into being contained more air within than matter, and could be rearranged easily and instantaneously, over and over again. Yet of all those cities, only Tangier—a port city, a gateway, an international zone inhabited since 500 BCE, aged with the iniquity of commerce—gave off the feeling that purgation was necessary, by fire made of that stone, with your skin to be cleansed by the friction of the ashes.

Once out of that city, the sense of corruption dissipated, but the kaleidoscopic nature of the experience continued. We drove inland—the French created a fabulous system of roads that have stood up well in the dry climate—toward the royal twelfth-century cities of Meknes and Fez. The twelfth century was the height of Islam, before the reactionary clerics united to decree that science was subject to the Koran and the imams' interpretations, similar to the endless war in the United States between science and "scripture." Not much later, the Spanish drove the Arabs back into North Africa and have only their architecture to remind them of a great period of human tolerance and achievement not equaled since.

On the plain between Meknes and Fez, we saw a Berber harvest festival involving a group of more than two hundred in traditional finery, with two competing companies of horsemen carrying banners, spears, sabers, and muzzle-loading rifles charging at each other, back and forth, for over an hour as the waning sun struck highlight after highlight from the steel, silver, and gold in their weapons, costumes, and even their faces. I saw one woman of about thirty with solid gold teeth burnished by the diminishing light, easily as beautiful as Ingrid Bergman or Catherine Deneuve, raptly attentive to the horsemen and their maneuvers. Then dark fell and they were gone.

Fez is the better city for tourists, perhaps because of its educational institutions and its age-old practice of crafts such as weaving, metallic sculpture, and weapons. Geometrical woodwork and furniture embellished with ivory, mother-of-pearl, metallic inlay, and semiprecious stones only touched the surfaces of centuries of patient labor. We were lucky to get an inexpensive day-long guided tour, featuring a fabulous lunch that included pastilla, the Moroccan pigeon pie enclosed in delicate pastry. This feast occurred in a second-floor gallery overlooking a courtyard in the Medina, the oldest and most complicated part of the city. Long before the end of the day I ran out of Kodachrome. So when we returned to our hotel I dashed out to purchase more, hastening back before dark to capture images I couldn't bear to be without, especially the skeins of dyed wool that hung across the higher floors of the narrow streets, most of them eight-hundred-year-old footpaths.

I carried the Michelin *Guide Bleu*, with its detailed map of all the streets in the Medina, some of which ran only ten or twelve feet before sharply turning or intersecting with another. Within five minutes I was totally lost, worlds away from where I had entered the maze, and had to pay (or at least did pay) a young boy the equivalent of three dollars to escort me back to my car. Though it took about a minute and a half, it felt like years—I am sure I could never have found my way out on my own. I was literally gasping for breath and soaked with sweat when I paid him and shook his hand in thanks, which seemed to confuse him, but the thanks were all too real.

Then southward to the Sahara, a long, increasingly sandy stretch, again with perfect roads, little farms, and not much going on except camels on the loose, and light and medium-sized trucks laden with produce and animals. Still some miles from the desert, we started to see the tops of royal palm trees at about the level of the ground's surface, which betrayed the life that was occurring in the wadis, or streambeds, which had been carved down twenty or more feet by small, consistent streams. At one point we stopped to see what lay below, which was astonishing and ordinary at the same time.

From the streambed to the wall lay houses and gardens, along with the palms, crammed in tightly and regularly on each side of the water. People were doing the things all people do every day, back and forth, although not much up and down. Not far away I spotted a man with a hoe weeding no more than a quarter acre of corn. He was wearing a white, short-sleeved bowling shirt from a UAW local in Detroit nicknamed "The Keglers." I wondered if he knew what the name meant, or even what bowling was. Then we drove on, reflecting on the rhythm of what we had seen—somewhere north of an adagio but nobody's allegro, to be sure, tempered as it was by the heat.

And now we were indeed at the desert, the endless Sahara, a tangible oceanic nothingness of infinite proportion, consisting of perpetual vanishing points receding from each other indefinitely. Just as the village in the wadi had struck us as almost Hobbit-like (a word I had recently learned), the few outposts of buildings seemed tiny here because of their overwhelming setting. We spotted what we figured was an inn, with caravans of trucks around it, that bore the sign "Du Roi de Biers," a name all residents of St. Louis would have chuckled at. Here it seemed doubly humorous, since France is better known as a temple of wines, while Morocco—Muslim and therefore teetotaling—offered this down-to-earth peek at tolerance far from the imams in their cities.

The reception area and front desk set the tone—early Antonio Banderas or Clint Eastwood—with a single layer of bricks serving as both facade and interior. My partner had done a year of college in Paris and my own French was restaurant quality (with a lower case "q"), so I unloaded the bags while she parlayed and, when ready, carried the luggage to our room down the corridor in the one-floor establishment. Our room was big and bare, with no decorations I can remember, and the shower was in the corner with a two-brick-high barrier jutting out from the corner's sides, meeting about four bricks out at a right angle. The room was equally hot and dusty, with an undercoat of sand, and it had been a long drive, so I ceded the shower to her. She turned both handles fully to the left and watched as water belched out and spun against the bricks, then down a wide, unprotected drainage hole.

Pulling off her longish T-shirt and throwing it in the direction of the bed, she did a sort of jeté into the midst of the spray, screamed, and leapt out within a second or so. Standing there dripping wet with her teeth chattering, she half-squealed and half-squeaked to me that the water was ffrreeeezzzing cold. There was no hot water at all. She grabbed a surprisingly capacious bath towel, slipped her panties back on underneath it, and jerked the door open, setting sail for the front desk a few meters away without pausing to look back at me.

As you can imagine, I was laughing inside while trying to

assemble a face of indignity verging on outrage. I was still dressed except for my shoes, but she had no shoes on, though in a joint like this shoes were pretty much beside the point, so off I went behind her. The desk clerk, not French by any stretch, was nevertheless displaying a frozen countenance in the classic pose that says, best in French but in many other tongues as well, "I don't understand a word you are saying, you rude woman, and even if I did I could not care less because there is nothing I can do about it even if I wanted to and I'm almost finished with my shift. Aside from which, there's an excellent Italian soccer game that's tied up and down to the last eight minutes, so *excusez-moi, s'il vous plaît.*"

My French is certainly wretched, but it was clear even to me that Barbara was shouting, over and over, "*Mais, c'est pas de l'eau chaud! Pas!*" as the clerk gestured à la Marcel Marceau to demonstrate that he did not understand, that there was nothing that could be done about it and/or—to the extent I could penetrate the thrust of his movements—that he had a hot date which would brook no interference whatsoever, or that his mother had just died. I knew I had to do something, so I bellowed, getting a good echo out of the low, unpainted plaster ceiling, "*No eau chaud! No eau chaud!*"

At this outburst he reached across the counter and grabbed Barbara's hands, which was not easy, what with her protecting the tucks at the top of the towel she had hurled together in her first frenzy and now could feel loosening due to her shouts. But he caught her off guard, gaining the element of surprise, and she instantly understood that this could not turn into a long conversation, so she just shouted "*Qué?*" or "*Qua?*" as loudly as she safely could, grabbed one hand back, and anchored it to the vulnerable side of the towel, thus achieving a perilous parity, if only for the moment.

The clerk spoke quietly and not too quickly, using an endearing tone of voice while looking directly (almost like a favorite dachshund) into her eyes. Later, she told me what he had said, which was, "Madame, when you checked in and signed the register, you must have noticed that the opposite page lays out our hotel's rules and regulations, which are part of our contract with you. You did not read them. I observed that, and know you are too much of a lady to try to lie about it. Now, among those terms and conditions, it states simply and clearly that all requests for hot water must be made at the time of arrival, since we do not maintain the boiler's fire mechanism. We live each day and night with enormous heat. The Sahara is not called 'the burning desert' for no reason. But you, Madame, did not specify '*l'eau chaud*' on your arrival, and therefore. . . ."

She pulled away, secured her towel more tightly, and asked whether he might kindly make an exception in this situation by accepting her apologies and stoking up the boiler so she could enjoy the hot shower that had surely been calculated into the large cost of our small and simple room.

Our clerk was devastated or, to use my favorite French word in all its splendor, "*désolé.*" Before my eyes, now that the battle had been secured, he had, in some slippery fashion, changed from a man who needed, more than anything, to confirm the recent expiration of his mother's life span, or else the hot-blooded nature of his heavy date, into someone who actually stopped and poured himself a glass of mineral water from a bottle heretofore concealed underneath the counter and took a long, slow pull on it before continuing.

Time was now his friend—his best friend, in fact. The boiler had been broken for quite a while, Barbara now learned, and the owners were debating whether to have a new part made from scratch, since the original factory had been long closed, or to undertake a larger expenditure and replace the existing unit with a new, or at least newer, one. Such was his power of persuasion that we found ourselves (oddly, to be sure) slowing down our search for the shower of our dreams and sliding, as into a slightly overheated bath, ever so cautiously, and starting to consider which of those two alternatives—as to the boiler, that is—would be preferable. But the fugue state didn't last, either, since Barbara ended it by asking, if this situation had been going on so long, what other people did in these circumstances.

We learned quickly, as he pointed out the door and across the street, that the Comfort Inn over there always had vacancies because of its high prices, but it also had a swimming pool, BLT sandwiches—which were not permitted at Du Roi de Biers—and a gas-fired boiler. He also observed that other prior customers of Du Roi did this despite the clear expression in the rules and regulations pertaining to our present situation that refunds of any type were "*interdit*," which means forbidden no matter how you spell or pronounce it.

All of this was performed in such a seamless, charming way that I thought about asking him to explain, before we left for next door, who had thought up this whole con job. If, however, you ask the dealer to show you how he pulled out that fourth ace when you knew there were three already showing, he will certainly be pleased to do that for you, but you will then find yourself under obligation to make a suitably handsome tip. So we cut our losses, packed our bags, and hoped we would, before too long, have a chance to profit from our expanded education.

It took a while, but it did happen. Taking a shortcut to Marrakech, we followed the *Guide Bleu* through the Atlas Mountains on a route shown as easily passable, which led us onto a narrow, winding, one-and-a-half-lane road carved about halfway up the side of a two-thousand-foot mountain. We ultimately descended into a small village similarly carved, with a gorgeous field of tall, tasseled corn along the river bottom below.

The road in front of the houses was the roughest I have ever been on. We crunched our way through loose cobblestone-sized pieces of pavement at about five miles an hour, which gave the village urchins a good deal of time to chuck some of those missiles at us. Luckily, the national sport being soccer rather than baseball or what we call football, and probably also because the village was so remote, and off any track that anyone but a halfwit would have chosen, there was little chance to practice, so they consistently fell short. This route brought us to a highway with a sign pointing to Marrakech, which somehow seemed like a traveling circus's winter headquarters. The famous square Djemaa el Fna displayed a wealth of performers and places to eat, outdoors and in, and its backdrop strongly resembled what we would recognize in a later decade as an indoor mall not unlike the one in Short Hills, New Jersey, or the Mall of the Americas in Minnesota. So we didn't stay long.

One highlight, though, was the city-block-sized, walled-in tomb of a previous royal dynasty, the walls being about twelve feet high and made of off-white stuccoed brick. A small anteroom featured an altar, with apparently perpetual illumination and several decorative objects on it, and opened into a garden with relatively modest aboveground stone tombs decorated with typical Islamic nonfigurative patterns in varying combinations. The dynastic tombs on the edge of the Sahara in Comfort Inn/Du Roi de Biers country had been surrounded by about three feet of windblown sand dunes and were not open for viewing, so this was, at the very least, an improvement—and turned into much more.

The garden held about twelve tombs, but the magic of the place came from the array of rosemary trees stretching above the height of the walls, planted closely like Lombardy poplars all the way around, and giving off about a kiloton of the most exquisite aroma I have ever encountered. The effect was concentrated, due to the little wind in Marrakech. Further, despite late September being the peak of harvest season, these were evergreens, so nothing had been harvested. The entirety, which was nothing short of majestic—not to say imperial—remained to honor those entombed in perpetual, heavenly fragrance. During the decades since then, anytime I have been near a stand of rosemary, I have been spun back to that place and moment, fully feeling the genius of the architect and gardener who conceived and built such a perfect resting place.

A long day's journey then took us to beautiful Agadir, which (based on the brochures) sits atop one-hundred-foot cliffs with walkways down to the Atlantic and spectacular, endless white sand beaches accoutered with beach chairs, periodic bars with awnings and wide varieties of refreshments and provender (mostly grilled, whether animal or vegetable), and infrequent lifeguard towers, but with comforting lifeboats stationed near each.

We had stopped for lunch in Taroudant, a wide place in the road that acted as the home of a huge camel market and featured a multitude of Tuaregs—enemies of Tarzan, if you recall—known as "Blue People" because of the indigo they use to dye all their fabrics, possibly so as not to be seen sneaking up on people during the night. Tuaregs believe in animism and are reclusive desert dwellers, slavers, and breeders of camels. After Marrakech, which felt in many ways created by Disney, Taroudant seemed genuine and handmade, the way you can tell a toupee from actual hair, or a machine-made oriental rug slammed out in Brussels from one woven by hand in Isfahan using the same method for a thousand years.

We bought some amber and had lunch on the second-floor terrace of an inn with a view of the markets. We were pleased with the rich and savory Moroccan cuisine, which contrasted with a family, *très chic à la français*, who sat next to us and ordered "Steak Frites" for all four of them. Unhappily, this move—obviously calculated to keep them on the safe side—resulted only in Madame's standing up and shouting at the waiter to ask if this was *bifteck* or *chameau* (camel). We headed off to Agadir before that question was settled to anyone's satisfaction.

Even with that interval, the long, dusty journey had us lusting for a dip in the equatorial Atlantic, so we were more than delighted when our hotel—staffed by French personnel, except at the arrival point and doubtless behind the scenes—provided us an oceanside room about ten stories up, making us laugh out loud as we pulled back the curtains. We eagerly jumped into our bathing suits and found the accompanying beach robes where we expected them to be, but no beach towels in the bathroom, the closets, or even the storage chests. Surely there would be no repeat of Le Debacle du Roi, not here in what to us resembled civilization more than anywhere else we had traveled through or stayed.

The front desk would certainly have the answer, we convinced each other, so off we sallied and down to that spot we went, full of confidence and *bon esprit*. The young man at the desk, natty as all get out in his tuxedo-like suit with starched white shirt and black bow tie, smiled at us in a perfectly French way—which is to say a bit, but far from fully toothy, that being seen as déclassé. Barbara's French had not really carried the day or even given us a fighting chance out by the Sahara, but it was, again, all we had to bring to bear on the situation. Perhaps the previous encounter had put a frog (*pardon, s'il vous plaît*) in her throat, or perhaps the *mien serieuse* of the desk clerk put her off her game. In any event, her French, after two or three introductory words, became her English, and the clerk was so thoroughly French that he couldn't understand a word she was trying to say.

Imagine that the following represents a tape recording of the actual event as Barbara once again assayed the local tongue. Barbara, speaking French: "But in our room there are no . . ." Desk Clerk: "*Oui, Madame?*" Barbara: "But in our room there are no . . ." Desk Clerk: "*Oui, Madame?*" Barbara: "But . . ." Desk Clerk: "*Oui . . . Madame?????*" She had frozen on the word for "towel." *Serviette*, as I was informed substantially later, proved to be the show-stopping term. But then Barb found a way to stop the back-and-forth. Barb, *à la français*: "Well, what do you do in your room after you take a shower?" Desk Clerk, with an Oscar-winning smile: "After a shower, Madame, you do whatever you please!"

The two of them dissolved in laughter—thankfully for me, since, until then, we were halfway down the toilet without even a towel, and I was well beyond the end of my rope desperate for a swim. But now we became the best of friends for the day, and she remembered the magic word. It actually turned out to be a concept rather than a word because, young as we then were, we hadn't realized that the critical items would be waiting for us at the bottom of the stairs to the beach, freshly laundered, fluffy as a Grand Marnier soufflé, and neatly stacked.

So, to sum it all up, our semi-safari into lightest, coolest Africa was a *vacance nonpareil*, with many things to see and none of the jihadist character of today. Plus, as the cognoscenti like to say, we learned two lessons that will last a lifetime. (Wherever Barbara is, even though we haven't seen each other for decades, I'm sure she remembers them, and this account is proof positive that I have also done so.) First, always ask about hot water before you sign the register—you'd be surprised how many times that has nipped the frozen shower scene in the second and third world buds. Second, after a shower, towel off and then, for goodness sakes, do whatever you please. Life is much too short to waste time considering the other options.

XXII   THE RADIOACTIVE RABBIT IN THE HATBOX IN THE CLOSET

THE LOBSTER in the story of Don Greene, Cameron Farquhar MacRae III, and Napoleon's penis was not the only lobster in the story of the law firm known as LeBoeuf, Lamb, Leiby & Mac-Rae, by a long shot. When senior partner Doug Hawes took a sabbatical in 1973 to teach law at a well-regarded school outside New York, he recruited a young woman named Susan, who had been first in her class, to come to the firm after graduation. When Susan joined the firm, she had just gotten divorced from her first husband, who had graduated a year earlier and later worked at Davis Polk & Wardwell, which was in the same building that LeBoeuf occupied, One Chase Manhattan Plaza. The entire top section of the elevator bank was occupied by the Wall Street Club (a tax-deductible men's "business club"), Breed Abbott, Cravath Swaine, Willkie Farr, Milbank Tweed, LeBoeuf Lamb, Davis Polk, and Reavis McGrath. I hope it's not out of place to note that some firms had nicknames, like Brer Rabbit, Milkweed, and, of course, The Ranch.

Doug was a person of substantial energy and charm as well as a good recruiter and business getter. His employment at the firm was courtesy, I was told, of a close connection through his brother to Roy Ferguson, the head of St. Regis Paper Co. St. Regis was one of the forest products oligopoly that is now smaller but most likely not very different from those days, and they had a boatload of anti-trust and corporate work that made them an "anchor tenant" of the firm's practice. I became Susan's second husband, and she is the mother of our wonderful children, so let's put that out there right away. The animal and vegetable kingdoms parallel each other in many ways, so the term "tree" is as useful for humans as it is for flora, although "vine" would be equally good, given the intertwining that proliferates in human stories, like this one.

So, the first parallel here is that after Susan and I intertwined, Doug successfully recruited another female associate, with whom he spent an enormous amount of time early on. I had the office next to him and never saw him devote so many hours with a single associate, hovering together over papers on his desk. It involved, he told me, a model set of bylaws, more than likely not billable. An ungenerous skeptic might well have wondered which set Doug was focusing on at the time. The new associate was blonde and extremely attractive, and her name was (and is) Ronda Muir, a good Scottish name. She was so readily noticeable that her nickname sprung full blown from Philip McGuigan's forehead, unofficial master of revels as he was at the firm under the tutelage of Paul Russell, his mentor. Paul was widely admired at the time for dating Julie Newmar, who played Stupefyin' Jones, the brunette bombshell in the Broadway production of *Li'l Abner*, but he later married the daughter of a Hong Kong shipping magnate, before dying in Bangkok of AIDS long after he left the firm.

Phil immediately dubbed her Ron Demure, an apt and ironic sobriquet, given that, while she was extremely well-mannered and cool as the coolest of cucumbers, she came across as the least demure of all the damsels aboard the good ship LeBoeuf. The final irony of Ronda (Doug did divorce his first wife and married a French countess he had met while attending many international securities seminars on the firm's nickel—to forage for business, undoubtedly, after Ronda left) was that she left because she married a partner at Davis Polk, where Cameron F. MacRae III had started, although Ronda's husband had also played a season or two for the New York Giants before finding the law a more congenial profession.

So in addition to the well-known connection between Dewey and LeBoeuf, there was a distaff bond of sorts between Davis Polk and our firm, involving extraordinary women. Ronda went on to greater glory by becoming, according to her Google profile, "Founder and Principal of Law People Management LLC, and one of the country's leading authorities on the personal attributes of lawyers and the application of behavioral science to the legal workplace," making a person wonder if that started when Doug Hawes smothered her with attention in the cause of developing the model set of nonbillable bylaws. Another of the numerous amazing women was Kimba Wood (later Judge Wood), primus inter pares, about whom we all know many wonderful and admirable things, who was then married to Jesse Lovejoy, also a partner at Davis Polk.

One thing we don't all know is that Philip McGuigan had an office close to her and would bellow out "KIMBA!" from time to time in the secretarial bay that adjoined their offices while pounding his chest in the "appropriate" gorilla-like fashion. His second act, as a '70s-style Upper East Side "swordsman," would be to regale the secretaries who constituted his captive audience with tales of his sexual exploits the previous night, which involved a variety of lovelies he had brought to their knees, literally, with his overpowering charm and manliness. Truly.

The firm was growing rapidly then, which precipitated our move across the way to 140 Broadway, but recalling the Christmas parties of '75 and '77 makes the evolution particularly clear. The first one, with Emily Cutler (later Essex)—as Randall LeBoeuf's secretary/assistant—actively involved in administration, we held in the basement of the Gramercy Park Hotel, on the north side, where Emily lived. The entertainment was provided by a middle-aged man who carried in his own keyboard, an early model of the type that produces drum, horn, reed, and synthesizer noises as well as piano. He only knew three or four songs, as we soon learned, the standout being "Proud Mary." He played that twenty or thirty times, since some of the young wags kept going over and asking if he knew it, and he, to show rather than tell, would play and sing it again. For a brief while, it became our song, Susan's and mine, because that event was where our romance began.

Two years later, the Christmas party was at a hotel on Lexington Avenue across from the Waldorf, in a large ballroom, with elevated cuisine and a real band. Since Susan and I had married in the meanwhile, and she was pregnant and Dave Bicks's masonry recommendation had torched our new co-op apartment on the West Side a week or two before, I missed the party. Nevertheless, I can profile the highlights briefly.

Our number included a secretary from an outer borough named LuAnn, who was young, quite slender, sunny, and highly competent. She also was popular with just about everyone, and married one of our partners some years later, after we had moved uptown to 520 Madison. The party was for lunch, with dancing and entertainment afterward, so LuAnn had arranged with her boyfriend of the time for him to pick her up on the 50th Street side of the hotel, after which they were to grab a quick bite and catch a show on Broadway.

The party, however, burst out with the kind of enthusiasm our parties often did, the alcohol flowed, and the dancing got better and livelier. I believe someone stepped up and paid the band to play for another hour, which fortunately was not a problem for the hotel, since they had plenty of time before their evening event. While the carousers caroused, the boyfriend waited dutifully downstairs inside the hotel entrance until finally, his patience more than exhausted, he came up to the ballroom. There he promptly zeroed in on LuAnn, dancing with two black guys, Harold and Robert, who ran our mail room, on the crowded floor. Our young Lochinvar dove right into the action, throwing several wild punches and precipitating a melee that actually caused very little corporal damage, because the onlookers turned quickly into peacemakers.

The china, however, was not so lucky. A large table laden with stacks of the hotel's best crockery tipped over, resulting in something like $10,000 worth of breakage, according to the word that got around. Two significant results ensued. The thin and lovely LuAnn became known, forever after, as "The Bone of Contention," for one. The other involved our head tax partner, Harold Seidel, and Cameron MacRae Senior. That one related (as many items involving Scotsmen do), to issues of cost and appropriate allocation thereof. There was no question that the hotel would get paid what it asked, which would be replacement cost. No, the question was deductibility. At bottom, was the breakage an "ordinary and necessary" business expense? Harold, in his puckish way, had his doubts, even in a firm where most partners ate many of their lunches together at fine gentlemen's clubs and deducted the entire amount of that enjoyment, because merely being in each other's presence made it clear that there was business on the menu.

MacRae had no doubt that the Internal Revenue Service would ultimately pick up the tab, and that any questions arising would be successfully negotiated by Harold. His reasoning was simple. The fracas was as ordinary as anything ever seen at an Irish, Polish, or hillbilly wedding, for a start. He was from western Virginia, so he knew wherefrom he spoke. Second, the necessity of the deduction (not the expense, but he hurdled that without breaking stride) was that it was the firm's money, not the government's, and that was it, sum and substance, although we never did go back to that hotel.

But what of Susan and the lobster? you ask. Wasn't that where we started? Okay. When Susan and I returned from our honeymoon in Paris and the Côte d'Azur, we came back to a newly purchased Central Park West prewar co-op apartment that had not yet been incinerated in the Dave Bicks fire, but for which we had planned some renovations. The first one was to take down the wall between the living room, on the west side of the apartment—looking over the roof of the Museum of Natural History—and the first bedroom so we could double the size of the spectacular view past the museum to the park and several prewar architectural masterpieces in that direction. Our super knew a man who specialized in this simple work. First, knock down the wall of thin cinderblocks with a sledgehammer. Then even up the ends of the former wall with the other attendant walls and *votre château est complet.* Since the man was non-union and had a weekday job, he would have to do this on a weekend, but it was a one-day task and the loud part would go quite quickly. Being a Seventh-Day Adventist, he didn't work Saturdays, so Sunday was his only free day.

We had returned, that Friday, to learn that part of the deal was for us to acquire a galvanized ten-gallon washtub, several bags of plaster and lime, four "corner beams," and a stepladder. Part of the scheme was for him to show up with only his bag of tools to avoid suspicion from the weekend staff, who were vigilant about keeping non-union workers at bay. So the next morning, Saturday, we rented a station wagon (this was long before SUVs), went to the recommended vendors to pick up the goods, hauled the stuff up to the apartment (which was half empty because we hadn't fully moved in yet), and got the super to come up and verify that everything was all set. He told us that the plaster and lime needed to be mixed in the washtub, then covered with a wet cloth overnight, so the plaster would be ready for the man to use when he arrived the next morning.

As it happened, we were due at an afternoon wedding and reception at the Plaza Hotel that same day, so we were more than a little nonplussed. Our super explained how to do the mixing, amazed that we weren't familiar with such a basic process, and assured us that we could accomplish the task quickly, after we returned from the reception and before going to bed. The wedding involved a former LeBoeuf secretary named Lisa Radoyevich—aka "Radish"—a delightful young lady whose father, Boris Radoyevich, was a stalwart Republican Long Island friend of Randall LeBoeuf, and a bankruptcy judge. Lisa had attended the Katherine Gibbs School of Secretarial Something and lived in a hotel solely for students attending Katy Gibbs. Through her father's set of connections, she had then immediately been taken on by our firm and put to work for Taylor Briggs. Radish was very bright, highly energetic, and an all-around "good scout," as the saying went. Boris's plan had obviously been to get her married into or through the LeBoeuf family, as it were. But he also had the good sense to convince her to join the Upper East Side Manhattan Republican Club, which was ultimately where she found her husband. Even better, that fellow provided her with a more appropriate last name, his own name being Tim Sweet.

I have never understood the expression about this being where the cheese binds, but it seems appropriate here, because part of Lisa's sojourn at the firm had included several sorties through the ranks of the partners: her boss, of course, but also several of the younger ones, including yours truly (for not that long—it was the '70s, remember). By the time Susan and I had recovered from the news on the plaster front, taken a half-hour nap to compensate for still being on Paris time, gotten properly gussied up, and managed to wrangle a cab to the Plaza, the tension had started to build. Susan had wanted to pass on the wedding, but I had remained a big fan of Radish and ended up with a genuine friendship with her (which lasted long past her wedding), so I was determined to go.

Our notion—the event being at the Plaza, and the East Side Republican Club being in essence the home team—was that we'd be offered a few cucumber sandwiches and modest canapés, perhaps deviled eggs, a couple of glasses of Long Island champagne, the wedding cake, and then off we would all go back to our individual hidey-holes. What ensued was otherwise. Boris laid it on thick and put all of Yugoslavia, as it then was, on display. Lots of hors d'oeuvres, champagne and wine, a sit-down dinner with Balkan delicacies and staples, plenty of potatoes, a steamship round of beef, and finally the cake. The dinner took hours, and we ate and drank our fill, having no alternative. But why would you want one? So we forgot all about the two lobsters and two bottles of champagne we had bought earlier that day—on our rounds through the world of interior construction—and that even now lay in our refrigerator.

Finally, we floated home, with darkness looming and very little lighting available in our apartment, getting grouchier with each flip of a light switch as we faced our remaining endeavor. We agreed the lobsters were a lost cause, acknowledging that Boris's noble repast had carried the day, got down to our skivvies, and started preparing the water, plaster, and lime for their amalgamation. In our state of exhausted and inebriated inexperience in this realm, and working in near darkness, we kept bumping into each other while lugging the bags around, only barely remembering to put a shower curtain down to protect the parquet in the entry hall.

Meanwhile, the focus shifted from our work at hand to how long Radish and I had interacted, what I had said to the bride during my turn on the dance floor, and so on, right down the hill with Jack and Jill. Finally, determined to finish this part of the job, I plunged my bare hands into the mixture, smoothing out the lumps and stirring vigorously to ensure that the plaster would move easily from tub to trowel to wall. Not long into the exercise, I felt the heat begin to build as I stirred and the chemistry of merger began in earnest. A huge amount of heat is released when you create the chemical reaction that produces plaster. By the time I was done, I had eight or nine half-dollar-sized blisters on my hands and wrists, which I then displayed with venomous pride to the woman I had promised not long before to love, honor, and cherish forever.

Dawn came, as it repeatedly insists on doing. The lack of curtains across our big windows facing the park denied further slumber, so we woke up, managed somehow to laugh about the previous day, and became friends again. The wall guy was due in a little over an hour, the timing designed to coincide with the neighbors' heading off to church or brunch if we were lucky, and we were starved. Susan is a great cook and we had done other provisioning of the refrigerator, so we headed out to the kitchen to fix some eggs and toast before the workman came.

First, we pulled out the bag with the lobsters, sure that they had perished and been rendered inedible. I put it down on the kitchen counter, and we looked at it, mutually sighing. Then something moved inside the bag, and it fell over, *Kerplunk!* We froze, but then sheepish, gleeful grins plastered themselves on our faces, followed by a whirlwind of water heating, lemon slicing, butter drawing, table setting, champagne popping, toasting the French bread and each other—which finally brought us, beaming from ear to ear, to tying each other's plastic bib from the fish store tightly in the back and sitting down to a return from a honeymoon in Paris breakfast that couldn't be beat, as Arlo Guthrie once notably sang or drawled.

Of course, this activity took more time than we had allowed, and the workman arrived when we were about halfway through eating. We took off our bibs, shook his hand, pointed at the wall to be removed, the corner beams (which were slender and twelve feet long, the height of the walls from floor to ceiling), the right angles of thin steel to make the corners of the walls flush and square, left him to his work, and returned to our breakfast. So we went on that morning, living our parallel lives, somewhat abashed that this man had come all the way from Brooklyn on the subway to see how people on Central Park West went about having Sunday breakfast—which always involved champagne, it would seem, and yes, delicious, fresh, fantastic boiled lobster at its best! Mel Brooks could not have done it better, although he probably wouldn't have done it that way in the first place.

———

But wait, as they say in the commercials for the triple-track storm and screen window sets, the Veg-O-Matics, the thirty-two various length sets of kitchen knives, and the easy-to-put-together various-sized sheds for your lawn tools, snowblowers, and badminton and croquet sets—wait, there's more! And it features the most famous lobster of all, at least in this context.

Susan is the product of your typical marriage between a

Sicilian doctor and a Welsh nurse whose father was a doctor. Of course, there is no such typical marriage, but theirs was a happy one.

When she was about nine, she entered her parents' bedroom in the middle of the night, stood at the foot of their bed—don't forget this was during the Cold War, when the specter of nuclear annihilation was constantly pushed in our faces to justify the "defense budget"—and awakened her parents with the news that there was a radioactive rabbit in a hatbox in her bedroom closet! She has always had a lively imagination and a strong ability to get attention, and she was truly afraid. They took care of it.

In the interval between our Christmas party encounter in the Grammercy Park Hotel and the honeymoon lobster homecoming extravaganza, a similar event arose. Our romance was still undercover and in its early months, and I had moved into her one-bedroom fourth-floor brownstone walkup apartment on West 70th Street in the park block. (Please read that sentence twice and figure out where to fit in the commas it must need, because I can't, and I want to finish the story.) The place was cozy, with a decent living room and eat-in kitchen, providing just enough room for two. Oddly enough, and through no doing of our own, we had been teamed up for several clients, one of which was Hackensack Water, where Adrian Leiby and Doug Hawes had put the two of us together. In this case, it was a first-mortgage bond deal, (there's that comma!) and we were due to go effective, price, and go to market the next day. Since it was something like the company's thirty-seventh first mortgage bond issuance, the deal had been straightforward; the players knew each other, and everything seemed to be set for a smooth launch.

In the fashion of that time, we left at the end of the workday, cabbed it over to the financial printer to finalize the prospectus and registration statement, assemble the package, turn it over to the printer to take to the SEC in Washington, trigger the effectiveness, and do the deal. Also in the usual way, the printers themselves always took a long dinner break around eight. That meant you would have no copy to review and sign off on, which meant in turn that the printing company would invite the lawyers, the company personnel (if any), and the investment bankers out to a nice dinner lasting around two hours, although usually a little bit more—the dinners were pretty substantial events, and since you were on the glide path by then, a good time could generally be had by all.

On this evening, we were taken to the Palm Steak House, which was about as good as it got. No one from the company was there. The numbers had been cleared, and all the fine tuning was in the legal end. It was Susan's first time at the restaurant. When she heard that lobster was on the menu, she perked up (not being that fond of beef) and showed a keen interest. With a lot of encouragement from everyone else on the team, she finally settled on their famous five-pound lobster. Susan weighed less than a hundred pounds herself at the time, so when the boiled beast was presented, she nearly fell off her chair, eliciting a huge round of laughter from the rest of us. Her dinner looked almost as big as she was. She was, however, true to her commitment, and demonstrated considerable energy and enthusiasm at her task while the rest of us munched our way through some powerful steak dish or other.

Dinner being done, and just the tidying up around the edges left, I played the partner role to the hilt and announced that I'd be heading home, and that Susan would cover the finishing touches. I hopped a taxi back to her place and fell asleep, full of comfort and the satisfaction of a job well done. At around two o'clock, I woke up as she finally appeared. She explained that one of the bankers, luckily, had done a last-time-around check and discovered a mistake in the financial table in the front. That error affected a lot of the numbers, especially the interest coverage ratio, on which the rating of the bonds rating depended. It was a glitch, to say the least, that had to be corrected or we had no deal.

The company was headquartered in Weehawken, New Jersey, in a tall building that was a perfect replica of the Palazzo Vecchio in Florence, at the top of the cliff overlooking the New Jersey entrance/exit for the Lincoln Tunnel, close to where Burr did in Hamilton, once and for all—until the musical, that is. The CFO, whose responsibility these numbers ultimately were, lived in suburban Connecticut, an hour and a half away from headquarters. When he got the call about the problem, he explained that his papers, which would yield the necessary information, were in his desk at headquarters and that the night watchman spoke only Italian. The call was over the speaker phone, and a universal groan met the news. But then the CFO laughed and said, "Relax and get a brain! My name is not Joe Pope for nothing. We parlez Italiano all the time, this guy and me." In those long-ago days, there was no way for our crew to do anything but wait and try to stay away from the printer's free, high-end hooch while the parlay went forward.

An hour went by in virtual silence. Then Joe Pope called and said he had a fax at home and would send down the correct numbers right then. Once checked, the new, corrected figures were set in place, the new pages cleared, and finally, finally, the package was checked again, signed off on, and the night was done.

All of this work, without computers and e-mail, is amazing to recall, and I'm not even sure how financial printers have evolved to stay in business. They were always hugely profitable—witness the tickets to championship fights, Triple Crown races, elaborate dinners, and "nights out on the town," which their salesmen proffered at every opportunity. When Susan told me the story, I recalled my first night of that sort, working for Dave Bicks on a GAC Properties Credit subordinated debenture issue. Dave's version of the deal might differ, but I ended up with a sense that GAC Properties had no trouble peddling its retirement real estate in Florida and Arizona whether it was above or below water, and also whether some part or other of the property might also belong to the National Park System or the Everglades or

Sonoran Desert State Park. But I'm sure controls and methods by which an appropriate margin of safety had been established were buried deep in the documents I hadn't really had time to read before being called in on printer duty. That night, Dave had the accountant in Miami, someone named Marty, on the speaker phone in a large conference room at the printer's. The "BarChris" case had just come down from the Supreme Court, and people had become antsy about accountants' comfort letters. Ours had not been finalized, so Dave was asking when it would be ready.

Dave and the accountant were properly matched: Dave very New York and authoritative, Marty down South perfectly evasive Miami, each highly comfortable in his own skin and speaking loudly so everyone could hear. It was nearly eight o'clock, which meant the two-hour dinnertime loomed, and Dave was trying to tease out of the accountant his commitment to when we would have "the number" we needed. Finally, after a soliloquy or two about the difficulty of his work and the various steps, checks, and double-checks it involved, Marty caved in, it seemed, and said, "Okay, I know I gotta give you something here, so I'm going to say we will have the number for you by ten thirty, maybe a little later, but before eleven." People around the table smiled and nodded enthusiastically, and then Dave responded, "That's great, Marty, so we'll be back by then for certain. Should we call you or just wait?" Marty was silent for a moment, and then he replied, "No, you just sit tight and wait. But Dave, I think I should tell you. It could be kind of an iffy number." The room erupted for a moment and then, as the noise abated, you could hear Marty laughing as he said, "I'm glad everybody's appreciating my sense of humor. Enjoy your dinner. Talk to you later." It's very hard to imagine that happening now. Very little Damon Runyon in the world these days.

But with this digression, I almost forgot the lobster, which is where we started and where we need to end. At about four thirty that morning, me having gone back to sleep for a couple of hours, Susan starts pulling on my shoulder, shaking me. I sit up and ask what the matter is. Her eyes are so wide open I can see their whites clearly in the darkened room. She looks frantic, like someone out of *Wuthering Heights*. Then she begins to pick with both her hands at something I can't see and nearly shouts "That thing. That thing. That thing." This is in a hundred-year-old Manhattan brownstone, so I voice the first thing I can think, "Cockroach? Are you talking about a cockroach?" She responds, almost sobbing, "No, the lobster. The lobster was supposed to be attached to the registration statement as an exhibit and I forgot to include it! I forgot!"

XXIII   THE GAME OF CLUE
WITH ALICE COOPER

HOT STUFF!! CAN'T GET ENOUGH!! Third-year lawyer, sittin'
in first class, my pre-flight champagne in a Waterford glass.
That's the way we did it in the long-ago past. I'd just come to
Chicago from Boston, where I closed a good-sized deal. Now
I'm heading for Hawaii—my first time, and that's for real. My
first chance to bill twenty-seven hours in a day, the White Man
Lawyer's dream!

Brand-new client, they gave me the assignment to put the oil
refinery in a state of alignment. Overnight at LAX, then catch a
dawn flight. To see Diamond Head the same a.m. will be a sensational sight.

That's the way I remember it, from back when rap was a thing
you got on the knuckles from Sister Siena in seventh grade. We
had a four-hour flight ahead of us, a decent night's sleep in the
airport hotel, and a dawn voyage to Honolulu. Then I'd meet the
new client team, we'd start a very large (to my mind) financial
transaction that was likely to bring me back again, hopefully
more than once. In these situations, I normally have a hard time
believing something is really going to happen before liftoff, but
it was hard to see how this baby could go wrong.

For a change, I'd arrived—on a connecting flight—much earlier than normal, and I was enjoying the relaxation. The deal in
Boston had closed with just barely enough time to cab out to
Logan and catch the first leg of my trip, with three minutes to
spare. (No TSA then!) From there on, I figured the connections
would be easy. I was almost ready to pull out my material on

the new client and transaction when four youngish guys who looked like scenery movers at a Broadway show or extras in a production of *Cats* or *A Chorus Line* walked into the first-class area. Over-the-collar hair, jeans, work shirts, and jackets in a variety of colors with striped knit collars and wristbands, and each with a different animal—dragon, lion, panda, fish monster—embroidered across the back. They reminded me of the jackets GI's buy in Korea or elsewhere in the Far East to wear on leave.

They settled into their seats, two in the center section across the aisle from me and the other two to their right by the far window. I was curious about them, partly because of their garb and partly because they were chattering and laughing. Then one of them pulled out an LP album cover, which they passed back and forth admiringly, taking their time to look it over. The one nearest to me had long, stringy, dark hair and a narrow face, while his neighbor had more of a sandy bouffant hairstyle, and when he turned toward me, I noticed his puffy lips and sultry, almost androgynous, look.

This group looked interesting, I thought, and tomorrow's long flight from L.A. would give me plenty of time to prepare for our opening meeting, which wasn't until the morning after tomorrow. Cycling through my options on how to start a conversation, I waited until one scrolled up that might give me a reasonable shot. Ultimately, I leaned across and touched the dark-haired guy lightly on the shoulder. He turned around with a wide-eyed gaze, lifted an eyebrow slightly, and waited for me to speak.

"You know, Keith," I started, "if you hadn't been sitting there next to Mick, I never would have picked you out! How about that?" From the way his lips moved, I could see that he was running his tongue around inside his front teeth before responding. Then he said, "That's funny. Are you funny all the time?"

"Just when I get the chance," I responded. "I made you guys out for funny when you got on. Wasn't I right?" When he replied "You were dead right, my new friend," and offered his hand to shake, I knew this flight was going to be much more entertaining than I had anticipated.

The captain and the stews got all of us organized for takeoff, and my new friend and I gestured about picking up the conversation once we were airborne. As usual, it took a few minutes to get to cruising altitude, when drink orders could be taken and dinner orders provided. He was having a martini to start, but my career as a corporate lawyer with a big Wall Street firm was not that far along, so I met him halfway by asking for a G&T. When the drinks arrived, we toasted each other and exchanged names. His was Alice Cooper, as in the Alice Cooper, the eccentric and comical rock star whose career of shock rock, heavy metal, and guillotine fakery has lasted more than fifty years.

We did a rapid-fire exchange of essential information, mostly about him—surprise, surprise—through which I learned that his father was a Presbyterian minister, that Alice Cooper was by no means his real name, and, most interestingly to me, that he had an early commercial version of a video recording and playback machine. The latter meant that his favorite thing at the moment was getting whacked one way and another, followed by watching the tape he'd had made for him showing (via now commonplace splicing) a series of events: four-horse photo finish/seventy-yard broken-field touchdown run/grand-slam home run/figure skater doing a triple Axel/buzzer-beating game-winning half-court basketball shot/knockout punch/diving center fielder's shoestring fly-ball catch/nine-horse disaster at Aintree as the field of horses tries to clear the last hurdle, a hedge with a ditch behind it—and on and on through a number of sports. Plus, you could rewind it again and again and again, and, further plus—there weren't any commercials to make you lose your focus in the middle of writing your next top-ten hit. "School's Out for Summer" was the band's only top-ten hit, but that's what you aim for if that's the business you're in, he explained to me.

Dinner came and was eaten. Alice turned back to his mates,

and they chatted each other up cheerfully, toasting along as we moved, pioneer-like, westward. Meanwhile, I tried to think how I could keep this priceless but soon-to-be-ended conversation/ experience going. Well, "Don't worry, baby. Everything will turn out all right" should have been my middle name or mantra (if I'd known that word), but this was no Beach Boys outing.

Less than thirty seconds after I'd hit a blank in terms of my next move, Alice wheeled out of his chair. On his way down the aisle, he grabbed my shoulder and said, "Hey, Funny Man— we're going to the upstairs first-class lounge to play Clue. You want to join us?"

Cruise control doesn't halfway describe it. I walked up in the band's jet stream, was shown my seat, next to Alice, my drink order was taken, and someone—Smitty the drummer, I'm pretty sure—instructed the stewardesses on how to assemble the cards for the game: three cards denoting location, weapon, and murderer in the mystery envelope, and the rest into the pile that everyone draws from, as in card games.

We played I don't know how many rounds, taking turns guessing what the right three-part answer might be—Mister Green did it in the kitchen with the rope is the proper formulation, but only if each element is correct. Over and over, we were wrong, which meant about five more rounds of drinks, on the airline. A sense of frustration descended that fit very poorly indeed with the spirit of the occasion and the game.

Finally, we were released from our earthly torment when Smitty threw his hand in the air and called a time-out. I learned later that his sister was married to the bass player, and if that's not a solid rhythm section, I don't know what could be. In any event, Smitty waved off the stew as she brought the next set of booze, and said, "Hold on, guys. I've got it. Colonel Mustard did it in the library with Miss Scarlet!" We immediately booed and balderdashed him, but he held his ground. He explained that we had tried all the other combos in various ways, and that was the only one that worked. All it meant was that our favorite stewardess had failed to understand the rules as Smitty had explained them. By then, we were prepared to be quizzical and for the game to be over.

Smitty did the honors, asking Darlene for the secret envelope and summarily dumping it on the board to reveal the brilliance of his insight. The deed had indeed been done just as he predicted, but instead of murder it appeared to be sex, of some brand or other. We breathed a huge sigh of relief, followed by the biggest laugh I have ever achieved anywhere, anytime. I got it by revealing that this development troubled me very deeply for one simple reason: I was planning, had been planning, to get married in about six months to a fabulous young lady whose last name was Sgarlat (pronounced Scarlet), and I had never come close to imagining that Colonel Mustard was anywhere in the picture, much less her type!

I have never seen Alice or the band since that flight, now decades ago. The next morning, licking my wounds from the previous night in the Ambassadors' Club at LAX prior to takeoff, I indulged in a restorative Bloody Mary before boarding my flight to Honolulu. The only other person at the bar was the great Patrick McGoohan, the original "Secret Agent Man" of '6os TV and an Oscar-nominated King Edward I of England in *Braveheart*, among many other outstanding performances. In my mind, he was then "the coolest of the cool dudes," and he remains so, two dozen James Bonds to the contrary notwithstanding. For once in my life I knew just what to do, which was to toast him from the far end of the bar, and have it reciprocated. No words were needed.

On the flight out, first class was almost empty, so I got to have lunch with the editor of *Barron's*, Alan Abelson, and his new wife, starting their honeymoon in paradise. As Wall Street insiders—now that I'd been doing deals for almost three years— we talked comfortably about fraud, rigged books, and fortunes gained and squandered. I also held up my end by telling, for the first of many, many times, my Alice Cooper story.

Coming back from a fabulously successful Honolulu trip, which led to another two dozen visits involving a wonderful client—the best kind, since the business was either expanding or trying to stave off bankruptcy—I stunned my beloved by suggesting that we accelerate the wedding and make it a small event with NYC friends and a weekend honeymoon in New Hope, Bucks County, Pennsylvania. My thinking was simple and based on experience. There are all too many Colonel Mustards abroad in the land, and very few pearls of great price named Miss Sgarlat. Amen.

XXIV SPECIAL DELIVERY

IT WAS A *quis custodiet ipsos custodes* situation if ever there was one. Who watches the watchmen? My partner and I were alone in the van, heading into lower Manhattan and headquarters. A totally crazy day, what with the drug raid, the fire in the apartment building, the FBI showing up out of nowhere, complete with TV and newspaper crews and the arrival of the AIDS bike-a-thoners passing through on the last leg of their ride down from Provincetown. Which was not to say that the two briefcases between us on the seat were anywhere but at the center of our consciousness.

"So?" Bobby had a way of making a monosyllable into anything from a primal scream to a chapter out of Thomas Aquinas.

"So what; so?" I was the talker and the deep thinker, and he was the man of action, which was why he was driving and I was lighting cigarettes for both of us. We could see the bicyclists on the West Side Highway, which was cordoned off, so we had to detour down Riverside Drive. We slowed up for the speed trap at the viaduct before you get to Grant's Tomb and waved to the guys in the squad car, catching their return wave in the rearview.

"So what do we do?"

Even though I already knew the answer, I waited long enough to show that I recognized it was a serious question. "Take a look, right?" Curiosity might have killed the cat, but I never had much use for cats anyway. The combination lock on the top case was set at 007. All I had to do was press the button and watch the catch fly open. It was as full as it had felt when the sergeant handed it to me. Hundreds, wrapped in rubber bands and stuffed and stacked, six by four. I'm no good at math—if I were I would have some other kind of job than the badge-and-gun thing—but you didn't have to be Einstein to figure out that it stood around a million. That was why they wanted it off the scene right away. Once there had been a fire in the apartment upstairs from mine. It happened while I was out running errands, and when I came back, my place had eighteen firemen in it and every one of them wanted to make sure I knew where my camera equipment was, if you understand the point I'm trying to make. So just imagine what two big briefcases full of cash at a three-ring circus like we just had driven away from could produce in the way of a sense of opportunity or exposure.

The other briefcase, when I managed to flip it over and get at it, was the same story. The only difference was that its lock was on 000. In a world where the small end of the ordnance is a .357, why dick around with a ten-cent combination lock, right? This one was full of twenties and fifties, older bills. That would be the customers' money. The other was for the suppliers, like bags of laundry, soiled and clean, incoming and outgoing.

"About one point one," I said. "Give or take." Bobby was quiet for a few seconds.

"Yo!" *Yo* was a word he never used. When he said it now, it contained a built-in exclamation point. If you could hear italics, this word had them. Not capital letters, italics.

"Did you ever see a fire drill like that one up there?" Being as I can talk and think at the same time, and that there is nothing more painful than a situation in which one person is thinking and the other person is waiting for the results of that thinking, it felt important to grease the wheels of social discourse. "Did you see Castro's shiner from when he tripped over his own feet and smacked into the post at the end of the second-floor stair rail?"

"Well, he's a dork and a backstabber. That's how he made sergeant. Serves him right." The questions in Bobby's silence now were different from his usual ones, like whether a certain female might be worth the trouble, or whether a certain individual walking down a certain street might be worth a certain amount of further attention to see if the telltale signs we both saw would translate into arrestable behavior in the next ten or fifteen minutes. The answer to those particular questions were usually no and yes, in that order, which was why we worked so well together. In a world of limited range, predictability rewards those who stick with the short odds. The questions this time were more open-ended, like if and how much.

Normal procedure involves a quick check of contents of property that gets confiscated, before you voucher it up. We weren't narco, just uptown cops brought in to support the Mighty Mouses as they swirled down with their capes wrapped around them and their cute tights. But all the hoorah that had erupted when we went in there, plus the presence of enough civilians to sell out Yankee Stadium, had put us in our current position.

The sarge would never forget that there had been two cases, but that was all he would ever remember. Too much incoming. We were from Inwood, the northern tip of Manhattan, so any extra time we took getting to our destination, as long as it didn't involve an overnight stay, wouldn't show up to create a problem. If you just picked up a couple of new cases three-quarters of the size of these items and restructured a little, that would be two hundred K apiece, free and clear, at least.

"Two hundred each, give or take. Any more than that, it's a problem." Bobby's answer to that was to take another drag and toss his butt out the window. I noticed he wasn't making the yellow lights the way he usually did. Like they say about the great athletes in crunch time, it all seemed like slo-mo. As I sat there, the only thing I wasn't weighing was if Bobby would ever rat me out. That would never happen. I could take that to the bank or the grave.

The addiction would be immediate. Like the crack it came from, it would be there now every minute of every day, every second of every minute. Why had I signed on for this gig? Because I knew I could do twenty years of anything, and in this case, twenty years would get me a pension, a chance to fish, work odd jobs, play golf with people I've known all my life, read some books, see my kids grow up and get married, spoil my grandchildren, dye my hair, and chase young girls if I got bored—or, if it came to that, write a letter to the editor.

It was that against the "if." If I did this, the "if" would always be there. The feeling of asking yourself—when you're out at sea and hauling in a nice-sized bluefish after a fight with it that calls for another glass of lemonade out of the cooler—if this would be the day a squad car would be waiting at the dock when you pulled the boat back in. To put that on top of living the next fifteen years one minute at a time, because it would always be there—the opportunity, the temptation, the calculation, the evasion, the self-justifying rationalization—every working minute, and end up with a life that hung from the word *if*, was for a stronger man than me. Or for one who didn't have a plan, which I did have, however stiff and simple. I laughed.

"No go, huh?" Bobby reached out and snapped his fingers for another cigarette, which I lit off the end of mine and handed to him, as I had done so many times before.

"No," I said. He knew I was right. That was part of who we were together. That was how we could sit for hours in a squad car and never say a word and never be even slightly out of synch.

"I thought so," he replied. "Yeah, I thought so." He pulled the van into the passing lane and pressed the accelerator. We would both need a beer sooner rather than later, as soon as we dropped our package. The part I will always remember best is his smile, a little lop-sided, when he looked at me then. "What a day," he said. "What a bleeping day."

XXV ROYAL AUTOMOBILE CLUB, JUNE 1914

SEVERAL YEARS BACK, I attended an Alumni Day at my college, held annually in mid-February, a wonderful way to split the dread month in half. The event traditionally begins with lectures by professors or speeches by distinguished alums, followed by a ceremonial luncheon honoring students of high achievement and alumni with distinctions of various sorts, and concludes with an extremely moving Service of Remembrance in the University Chapel.

I chose to attend the talk in the largest classroom, about half full on that day, on the origins and key issues of World War I. The subject had been of perpetual interest since our one-time university president later became the U.S. president who won reelection with the slogan "He kept us out of war," though once it was clear that the Romanovs had moved (as subject matter) from politics into history, he promptly got us into war because of the Red Menace of socialistic Communism. The "new" movie *1917* nails its future relevance.

Our lecturer brilliantly boiled down the essence of that war. On the Western Front: too many soldiers, too little room for battle, east to west, thus causing the north–south dimension to be soaked, resoaked, and resoaked again in blood. As for the Eastern Front: endless miles of battle lines and very few soldiers, plus a combination of mountains and vast, empty plains, resulted in forays encountering few enemies and no positional change whatsoever.

The speaker begged our indulgence to share an anecdote he had been witness to—not during the war (he paused for the laugh he was due for that), but at the retirement dinner of the longtime Washington, D.C., bureau chief of *The Economist*. On June 28, 1914, when the honoree had just started working for the magazine, everyone who seemed to be anyone had gone abroad for the running of the French Derby at Chantilly. There was a vast silence in London, traffic-wise and news-wise, so an older colleague invited him to come along to the Royal Automobile Club for a swim and a "spot of lunch" afterward.

The only other person in the pool happened to be Winston Churchill. Go figure that! They exchanged nods, and all went about their business. Then the two journalists climbed a flight to the dining area and stopped for a moment to check the teletype machine at the top of the stairway.

His friend picked up the tape and scrutinized it with a frown. When he turned to his companion, he sputtered, "Wouldn't you know it! Archduke, Assassinated, Sarajevo! And not a bloody English horse for win, place, or show!"

XXVI NIGHT COURT

MY GOOD FRIEND PHIL, a math-whiz classmate from college, used to walk around our small campus wearing a tweed jacket, turtleneck, and cavalry tweed slacks, and carrying a shoulder holster with a Walther PPK automatic handgun. He kept a boa constrictor in his room, which was a "single" if you didn't count the snake.

After law school in New York, Phil started to write spy novels in a series based on James Bond. The James Bond novels established the gold standard in that genre, to be sure. The Matt Helm spy novels (remember the movies with Dean Martin?), which were derivative of the Bond works, came next. Then came my friend's versions, which were knockoffs of the Helm capers. When I found out he was using the pen name Chase, I promptly deduced—which he acknowledged—that his plan was to get on the bookshelf between Raymond Chandler and Agatha Christie. His work had a propensity to go high and low at the same time, so that an international conference about the law of the sea would lead directly to a fictional threesome involving African, Nordic, and Brazilian participants, two of whom later died, one strangled by—yes—a boa, with a denouement at Windows on the World.

Later he graduated to the Scott Turow–style courtroom dramas with murder as the subject. A definite step up, these earned him considerable chunks of change, with paperback top-ten best-sellers and one that got excellent reviews and even sold well in hardcover. His puckish sense of humor led him to put my last name second on the letterhead of the law firm where the defendant was also a senior partner, and to give all the characters in one book first and last names of dorms and classroom buildings at the university we both graduated from.

This story actually begins when he called me up to cancel our usual lunch, something we did four or five times a year, because the chief of the criminal division of the Manhattan DA's office had found an opening in his own lunch schedule for that same spot. "I have to go, you know," he said. "He doesn't get free that often, and God forbid I should have to make up these stories for the books myself."

Then, two weeks later, he called in the afternoon and asked me to have drinks with him at the Players Club on Gramercy Park (founded by Edwin Booth, brother of John Wilkes), and then go on to dinner at the National Arts Club for the quarterly meeting of the New York chapter of the Mystery Writers of America. Our host for drinks would be a good friend of his who had been awarded several Edgars, the mystery writer's Oscar, and was a favorite of mine. I gave him a quick yes and the game was on. Both the famous writer and the Players' Club, with its portraits of famous actors and stage paraphernalia, were outstanding, but dinner was otherwise.

I had expected lively repartee about plots, methods of murder, oddball protagonists and villains, and detective procedures I could pass on to family and friends, but the talk was all about rotten agents, lying publishers, getting cheated on royalties, shelf space, advertising budgets—a perfect snoozeroo! I felt a little let down as we departed, but then Phil said that our mutual companion was working on a book that involved an extensive episode in night court, and had never been to a session, so he wanted to go down to Foley Square and watch some of the proceedings. Did I want to go? I was newly divorced and at loose ends, so anything seemed better than going back to my bachelor digs and having one or two more drinks I didn't need to help me get to sleep.

We taxied down. With three of us in the cab, the level of conversation lifted—we had the dinner and our companions to dissect and patronize in the way one almost always does after a gathering with strangers. I had come straight from the office, with my attaché case and camel hair overcoat, suitable for the season. Thus, because I was the one practicing lawyer in our group, I led the way up the stairs and into the building. The lobby was empty except for a folding cafeteria table with plastic bowls to empty your pockets into and a metal detector to walk through, as several bailiffs or officers of the court, wearing navy slacks, white shirts, ties, and gold-looking badges, manned the station.

The first man behind the table was a solidly built black man of about forty-five. As I put my case down and started emptying my pockets, he leaned toward me with a funny smile and said, "Would you by any chance be a lawyer?" I laughed, responding that he shouldn't let my camel hair coat, Brooks Brothers attaché case, and Paul Stuart suit, shirt, and tie mislead him, and we both chuckled. Then he asked, "Would you happen to be a lawyer named John Michael Parish, by any chance?" My jaw literally dropped. He exclaimed, "Harold Johnson, man! How are you, Mr. Parish? So good to see you," and we both zipped to the end of the table and engaged in a vigorous bear hug.

Harold had been the head of the mail room at the law firm I was part of for more than twenty years, when I first got out of law school. He was a delightful guy, full of energy and good cheer, very competent at his job, and respected by both the staff and the lawyers. He became part of our basketball team—don't be surprised if I told you he was the only "non-white" player, although more than one opponent snickered when they saw him play, asking me if that was the best we could do in the way of a black ringer. But Harold was lively and fun, and no one on our team ever regretted having him with us. I had lost track of him over the years, and I now learned that he had earned his college degree at John Jay, the police university sponsored by the city, and gone into the civil service. I told him he looked great in his uniform, and we slapped each other on the shoulder as I introduced my friends and told him about our mission.

We got the deluxe tour. He introduced us to everyone all the way into the courtroom, told us who did what, then wished us well, and said he had to get back to his post but how great it was to see me again and meet my friends. We settled in to watch. It was a quiet moment, so the judge picked up her hardcover copy of *The Joy Luck Club*, and we eyeballed various detainees, sitting together and surrounded by real cops, and speculated about the goings-on until the door burst open and about thirty "ladies of the boulevard" bounced in, cuffed and linked together with several long chains. They were singing and doing a conga line as best they could. Their dresses (if you could call them that), makeup, giant hairstyles, and high heels made for a lively downmarket Copacabana event as the policemen led them up in front of the judge, who put down her book, took off her glasses, and leaned forward to hear the assistant DA of the evening read off the charges.

That was enough excitement for our gang. We thanked Harold on the way out, as he and I gave each other one more hug and a high five, with no idea that I'd be back in less than three weeks. I did forty years of corporate law with major Wall Street firms and appeared in court fewer than ten times, always as co-counsel with a real litigator, to keep him or her on track with the facts. For more than one reason litigators are said to have "bathtub minds," meaning that they pour the facts of the case into the tub, which represents what they know of the law and courtroom tactics, and when the case is over, they pull the plug and start over. So when they stumble over whether they are trying a merger case or an air-rights conflict, someone has to make a hand motion, of either the two hands interlocking or linking thumbs and fluttering fingers, like birds do when they do anything interesting.

But once again, my life proved to be what happened while I

from the message, so Marc was hopeful that I could do the same fine job he had come to expect from me.

The kids and my future ex agreed that I needed to reschedule the overnight and leap into action, on the condition that I tell them the whole story once the trouble had been resolved. I was downstairs in the subway nearby in fewer than five minutes and popped up at Foley Square about twenty minutes later, as the dark was just beginning to descend on the city. I walked across the square to the courthouse, where my lucky charm, Harold, was standing in front of the lunch wagon out by the curb, paying for his sandwich and 7-Up and pocketing his change. Catching him before he could turn around, I gave him a strong but tender shoulder rub on both sides of his well-muscled neck, leaned forward, and whispered in his ear. "So good to see you again, my man. This time we've got some work to do."

No hugs or high fives this time—he had something in each hand and I was already pushing him up the steps. In we went, whizzing through the metal detector and down the hall, where he introduced me to the clerk of the court and showed me how to fill out the necessary forms for entering an appearance and being recognized and accepted as an attorney and counselor-at-law in the State and County of New York. In a remarkably short period of time, he also had introduced me to the head bailiff, who conferred with a junior bailiff, who then retrieved Marc from his holding cell. I shook Marc's hand and hugged him. Before we sat down, the head bailiff took me by the shoulder, saying that the assistant DA on the other side of the courtroom would like a word from me first. I pulled out my business card, handed it to him, said I'd be right behind him, and motioned to Marc to be seated and hang tight until I could talk with him.

I doubt that any ADA looks forward to a Night Court assignment, where you are likely the best-dressed, best-groomed person and probably have a considerable amount of trouble understanding what most of the other people in the courtroom are trying to say. This gentleman fully fit the picture. As I

was making other plans. Stopping by my old apartm
up my children for an overnight, I received a call fror
saying I had an urgent voice mail. When I dialed in,
message from a colleague and close friend of one of n
clients, an interesting character who had sent me a l(
and with whom I had an almost brotherly relationsh
Marc's funny bone should have been, as in my case,
wild and crazy bone instead, and the deals were alway
different. One instance afforded me a stay in a Holid
downtown Jackson, Mississippi, where, on the way do
elevator to breakfast, I met for the first and only time
a young adult wearing a floppy straw hat, no shirt or sl
newish overalls, suspenders cross-hitched in the back. (
enough, but it was memorable.

Marc was an investment banker who started at Gol
ter a Harvard MBA. Before that, he majored in pianc
counting and served as a walk-on member of a basketh
that went to the Final Four and lost to either Larry I
Magic Johnson's team in the semi-finals. He was six foo
athletic, with cafe au lait skin and blue eyes. He once
about going home from his firm's Christmas party wit
of the women from there, making—it had already beer
night—two dear friends and one permanent enemy. That
be all the background you need, except that while at Har
had shared an apartment with four female classmates fror
America. He ended up years later married to the one fror
ico, whose father was one of the twenty-nine richest Me:

This time, the message related, Marc was in Manhatta
tral Booking, which meant the Tombs, adjacent to Night (
and needed to get out so he could show up for work th
day. It was crucial that his employer not find out about th
needed help not only in getting released, but also in co
up a cover story and finding a "Real Lawyer," who could
all this mess go away with minimal consequences. The inc
involved property damage but no third party, I further lea

approached his desk, he held out my card between the fingers of his left hand and twanged it with the forefinger of his right, stopping for a moment to shake my extended hand while he said, "LeBoeuf, Lamb, Leiby Ampersand MacRae! Well, how-dee-do, Mr. Parish and company. I don't quite know what to say. You know we get very few PRIVATE COUNSEL in these chambers. How may I help you?" Actually, he was very civil and helpful, agreeing right away to release Marc into my custody and getting the judge to set a return date I could pass on to the Real Lawyer who would do the Real Lawyering. After signing the papers he put in front of me, I surveyed the courtroom before returning to collect Marc and noticed that the ADA, yours truly, and a pallid thirtyish-looking man in an olive green raincoat were the only people not of color. Marc told me on the way out that the latter was an airline pilot who had fallen behind on his alimony and child support, and nobody's happy camper at that point because he'd just missed his flight without being able to contact the airline and was sure he would lose his job now on top of everything else.

We sat down several minutes later in a dimly lit Italian "red sauce" joint two blocks from Foley Square. The City never sleeps, and neither do its constituent parts, lawyers and clients included, along with cooks, waiters, bartenders, and cloakroom attendants, known as hat-check girls in times that were both worse and better than our own. I ordered a large Pellegrino and a bottle of red not enshrouded in straw or pluggable by means of a candle and looked at Marc. I hadn't stopped to see what the charges were—that would occur when it occurred—and simply said, "Are we having fun, or what?"

He took a healthy drink of his water, looked me in the eye and replied, slowly, in his North Side of Chicago accent, "You are the Dog. No. You are the Super Dog! How did you get that done so fast? I thought I'd be there for a week, like that poor pilot chump. And when I finally got out, they'd give me a shoeshine box and a subway token!"

"A," I said, "I acted like I knew something, which I often do, in fact, although less and less frequently, and B, the subway token went out with Lindsay, almost before you were born. Why are we here? Did you do something? Does someone want to get you for something you already did, or were going to do, or he or she thought you might possibly do if you got the chance? Whose wife did you screw? Whose expense account did you countersign without looking at the bar bill from the hooker establishment? Fly high as the night—but you're still a crow on probation. Look at the menu. How might I help you at the moment? Give it to me, baby. I know it's going to be good. It always is with you."

We were done with dinner by the time he finished his saga, so here's the boiled-down version. After his kids were born, his wife—the Mexican heiress with the MBA from Harvard—decided she was bored and wanted to get back into the action of the business world and run something of her own. They had a live-in nanny, so she poked around and decided a travel agency looked good because there were a lot of travel benefits and not too much heavy lifting. They located a veteran of the business, a guy who even helped them find a good location on 14th Street, close to Union Square but also to their home in the West Village, to operate out of. Marc devoted his latest bonus to the project, and they were off and flying.

Marc was a free-wheeling guy, as noted previously, and believed his wife knew about and accepted the so-called 300-mile rule, which claimed that any infidelity committed on business trips, especially with stewardesses and waitresses, was outside the marriage contract. When she found out, as she inevitably did, she put some new juice into the concept of reciprocating. The night before last, his wife had been in Chicago with her second-in-command checking out hotels and restaurants in connection with putting together a package group tour. As Marc sat in his armchair watching a sports event on TV, he was overcome by an uncomfortable feeling that led him to the 14th Street office, then to her desk and computer, where he found conclusive evidence that she believed the 300-mile rule was as much sauce for the goose as for the gander. The crowning blow was the e-mail reminiscing about their night in the Warsaw Hilton, where she realized she had never known there could be so many uses for KY jelly!

Marc lost it. He found a hammer in a tool kit and smashed the computer monitors, opened the extensive wet bar and threw liquor bottles all over the room, breaking the bottles and anything they hit, overturned chairs, tipped over file cabinets, and demolished whatever else he could as a very fit and athletic forty-year-old. Then he took a cab home, poured himself a substantial scotch on the rocks, sat down in his chair and knocked back a large slug.

Before he could even feel the burn in his belly, a scream rang out on the street right outside his living room, a woman calling frantically for help. He jumped up, rushed out the front door, looked down the street, and saw, no more than thirty feet away, a woman being manhandled by two good-sized men. He ran up behind the one with his back turned and clouted him on the side of his head, knocking him down, his head hitting the sidewalk with full force. The other one had a firm grip on the woman's handbag and was shoving her with his free hand, which offered Marc a perfect target for a haymaker right in the kisser and a kick in the ribs for each of them to make sure they stayed down.

"It's okay, hon, it's okay," he said to the woman, wrapping his arm around her and stomping on the knees of the assailants to further neutralize them. (I did tell you he was from Chicago and played in the Final Four in college, right?) Everything flashed by in an instant after that—he recognized the woman as his upstairs neighbor, a squad car showed up in record time, he gave one of the cops the recap and their info to follow up, they were allowed to return to their building, and he escorted the lady, who was still crying and hugging him and thanking him for saving her. He saw her to her door, they had a big hug, and he patted her shoulder and went back to his scotch.

But after that lightning bolt of adrenaline, the alcohol had no appeal. He felt like he was on fire and had to "do something." There is truth in the maxim "In times of stress, we often regress," and Marc did just that. He grabbed his Burberry trenchcoat (standard issue for Wall Street types), went outside, hailed a cab, and went back to the scene of the crime. As he told me, all he could think of was that there must be something in the travel agency he hadn't broken, and he very much needed to take care of the omission.

The building's super had been awakened from his early slumber by the noise on the second floor, so as Marc walked in, he was greeted by that man and four cops and two plainclothes detectives. He looked at them, opened his arms, and said, "I did that"—one of the few available lines that gives an attorney zilch to work with.

Once he reached the holding cell in the Tombs, things got much better. Except for the pilot with the alimony problem, he was the only one there wearing more than a thin jacket. His Burberry spoke for itself, and when he told his story—still pumped up—he got nothing but sympathy, including one guy who said he'd like to "take your wife out, just to stay in practice," an expression that got a resounding "YEAH" from the others. For whatever reason—the time being about four in the morning or his A-list wardrobe—the cops had failed to discover his cell phone. There was a pay phone outside the cell, but the line was endless, and few had any money.

He offered his phone for everyone to use, after he had left cryptic messages for his wife and the kids' nanny and put out an SOS to his friend, who had called me. Marc knew he could simply call in sick, and did, for a day.

Then he curled up and caught some z's. You know most of the rest already. The ADA released him into my custody, and the next day I got one of my partners, a former assistant U.S.

Attorney in Manhattan, to represent him, and my own go-to guy worked out an ACD—Adjournment in Contemplation of Dismissal. That means if you keep your nose clean for two years or so, the docket is sealed forever, and everything goes away. A perfect ending to the nightmare. Marc's bonus several years previous had paid for the setup of the beloved travel business. And if one thing is true in America, it's that property trumps (pardon the expression) everything else, and that it subsumes the right to destroy it pretty close to however you want, as long as you don't destroy someone else's at the same time. Antique stores say, "You break it, you own it." This was vice versa.

Sometime later, Marc told me that a producer friend was wanting to make a TV movie about the incident. He was considering Denzel for his role and wondered who I thought should play me. I said either Woody Allen or Kevin Costner, but the movie never got made.

Nobody but a George W. is born on third base and believes firmly he hit a triple to get there. So I want to acknowledge the enormous leg up I got from my dear friend Phil the author, and from the rock-solid Harold Johnson, hopefully retired and playing pick-up basketball in some gym. Marc and his wife divorced with reasonable friendliness. Both were clearly ready for a change, and they loved their kids. Also, both were well-off, well-educated, and (as MBAs) not troubled by being cold-blooded about the whole contretemps.

Even more, I want to thank my best client ever. After one telecom deal, Marc threw the after-party at a blues joint on Rush Street in Chicago where we danced until 3 a.m., slapping high fives and doing spins I still can't believe I pulled off, laughing like happy fools. Without Marc, there would have been no story for me to write.

XXVII STRING THEORY

WE ALL REMEMBER the cat's cradle, both the string thing you can make around your fingers and thumbs, and the one in Vonnegut's best book, which involves a compound called Ice 9 that envelops the earth in the same way that the strings surround and occupy your fingers, making either or both unable to do anything useful. Physicists created the concept of string theory to try to mesh quantum mechanics with Einstein's general theory of relativity, uniting our existing theories about the way things work in nature at the smallest and largest levels.

Several years ago my college roommate's advisor shared a Nobel in physics with two other people for showing how gravitational waves caused by planetary collapse can be detected millions of light-years away, thus confirming an element of Einstein's theory that had lacked evidence. No evidence whatsoever supports string theory, but it remains a preoccupation of most physicists today. The same roommate during our undergrad days was looking for a piece of tungsten wire to complete an apparatus he was constructing for an experiment on a Saturday, when we had no classes. As he searched for someone who might know where to find such, he ran into a tall man with rimless glasses, short beard, tattersall shirt, and club tie and asked him if he might know.

"Haven't the foggiest, old bean," the visiting professor said in a plummy Oxbridge accent. "Theorist, you know."

I have no idea how long it took Einstein's theories to be proven by evidence. That's the big side. On the small side, quantum mechanics cost millions of dollars and innumerable hours of the time of brilliant mathematicians and physicists to find the Higgs boson and apparently conclude the search for final proof of the theory's correctness. Nor is it apparent to me that string theorists do anything but theorize, and there are no string experimentalists, although there is always, as we know, plenty of string.

The reason this comes up is that I recently went to a college reunion. It was an off year—that is, not a zero or a five—but I am the class secretary, write the column in the alumni mag for my class, live nearby, and was in the course of getting my final divorce, so attending seemed like a better way to spend my time than anything else I could think of. We reune in June, the weekend before commencement. Through the years I have had numerous wonderful conversations over a beer or more with seniors who will graduate the following Tuesday. Plus, every quad has two bands at night, so you hear great music, sometimes even by famous acts like the Beach Boys and the Neutron Bombers (no, I made that up) and even Ray Charles, way back when in space and time. So there I found myself on Friday evening, modestly beered and wondering what to do about dinner.

I noticed a line of people gathering and waiting patiently between me and my class's reunion. Most people, especially during off years, come on Saturday and go home late or stay over, and Friday is pretty quiet, filled with events involving major reunions to which off-year alums are not invited. I hadn't seen any classmates I might join for a meal, and the smell of grilling meat began to invade my consciousness, as wisps of smoke started to appear toward the front of the line. So I moved slowly to the end and fell in. You might note that it's hard to fall into a line, but that might be the key to solving the riddle of string theory.

The reason I make this observation is that the line consisted of members of the university orchestra, who were playing later that evening, and the meal was being held prior to their final rehearsal. So I learned from the gentleman in front of me, who was their principal oboist—player of the instrument known everywhere as an ill wind that no one blows good—and was getting his PhD in physics the following Tuesday. When I asked what his dissertation was about, he responded in a nano-second, "String theory."

I read *The Economist* every week, at least a reasonable portion of it, and had just read, several weeks before, a long article on that very subject. Peculiarly enough, I had also found in *The New Yorker*, about a month previously, a more quizzical piece on the same topic.

This is great, I said to myself, I'm loaded for bear on this baby. I did recall that the latter magazine had referred to this area as eligible for Bush W capital infusions, given that the absence of experimental data—they were still working on and arguing about what experiments might be most useful—could easily allow it to be categorized as a "faith-based initiative," and as I told him so, he chuckled mildly.

Continuing my efforts to look like a musician entitled to the burgers and franks being cremated up ahead of us, I pulled another factoid out of my bag of tricks and said, "It must be difficult to work in eleven dimensions." He chuckled again and remarked, "We've decided now that it's thirteen!"

"How wild," I replied. "So what are you guys playing tonight?" By the time we discussed that, we had been served our food. He went over to his fellow reed theorists, and I haven't seen him since. But in recent days, while thinking of true stories I wanted to tell you, this one occurred to me, and I decided to deepen my knowledge of the material on string theory—no, it's strings of words, but not otherwise. And what I found astonished me.

Quantum mechanics posits that, at its most infinitesimal, "stuff" is either a wave or a particle. Therefore, we have such specialties as particle physics and wave mechanics. But, string theory holds, you can never be sure whether it's one or the other at a particular time. That is why Schrödinger's cat may or may not be alive, and why Heisenberg, when he was alive and still now, will always be uncertain. When I was in college, my favorite bathroom graffiti was "Heisenberg may have been here." Not even he himself knows for sure.

What I learned is that a "string" is most precisely described as an infinitely long particle. Minds as simple as mine would call it a wave, but I honestly do not have the math to know whether that works, or whether it violates every known principle. I have also determined that at the time I was speaking with my oboist, there were still, in string theory, only eleven dimensions, not thirteen. I then deduced that he was, as we say, having me on, in the way that college humorists are drawn to do, by letting me know (when I figured it out) how much more he knew than I did.

I think I win this round, however, since I have figured out—remember the cat's cradle—that the entire field of string theory arose one afternoon, during a meeting at MIT or Caltech of math and physics wizards, when one of the senior members whipped out a bit of string from his pocket, said he'd been thinking about deep physics, and then conjured the cradle itself and asked his colleagues, "So, what do you think about that?" With that, they had all the evidence they needed, but they are still trying to work out the knots in the theory. Please read the first paragraph of this story again.

XXVIII LOS ALAMOS AND NEW JERSEY ITALIAN EPISCOPALIANS

WHEN I LIVED IN NEW JERSEY, my best friend was Jim Bay-ersdorfer, a retired Teaneck detective I met in a short-story workshop at the West Side YMCA in Manhattan fifteen years or so ago, before I moved to California. Jim is the most left-wing cop I ever met—happily not having met many (cops, that is). Like all cops, he has a million stories from his days on the force. He lives in a blue-collar town near the GW Bridge, spelled like the capital of Colombia but pronounced, with typical Jersey finesse, Buh Goat Ta, with emphasis on the middle syllable. To put things in perspective, the former mayor of Bogota, a blind right-wing Republican, rented a billboard to excoriate McDonald's for running ads and putting up signs in Spanish, and was soon after exposed for employing illegal immigrants to do work on his own house! Jim has had a tough life, starting with when his father died on a treadmill taking a stress test to get a life insurance policy for his family when Jim was four and his brother was eight. He got his college degree when he was in his early fifties after years of night school. Now that he's retired from the force, he works for a tree service, doing estimates, working on the crew, taking the wood from the trees they cut down, and splitting it up to sell out of the back of his pickup in the West Village on Saturdays and Sundays. He delivers wood to Harrison Ford, Annie Leibovitz, and other luminaries, and also has a list of older customers for whom he schleps the wood up three, four, and five flights in the old townhouses that populate that part of Manhattan. Part of what he carries around with him is the vivid recollection of two friends who were killed in front of him, the first when he was six and sledding and his buddy was hit by a car, just after Jim had made the slide down the hill and across the road near the Hackensack River. The second happened on the job several summers ago, when the tree services climber fell forty feet from a tree and landed on his back on the sidewalk right in front of Jim, who was helping on the crew.

I recently went to visit a college classmate who served for a number of years as director of physics at Los Alamos, a good friend I've stayed in touch with over the years. Damon Giovanielli was always one of the funniest people I ever met, as well as one of the brightest. He married someone named Ellie, and it's characteristic that when they met at a college mixer, he immediately decided she was too tough for him and he would never get anywhere with her, and she decided he would be more trouble than he was worth, so for five years they fixed each other up with friends until finally they faced the inevitable and ended up married, producing two daughters who graduated from Princeton and too many grandkids to count.

Also characteristic of Damon is that when Edward Teller, the father of the H-bomb, came back to Los Alamos for a commemoration of that event, he asked that Damon introduce him. This is not as simple as it sounds, since Teller was the man who most notably claimed that J. Robert Oppenheimer (known to all as "Oppie"), the progenitor of the Manhattan Project and the patron saint of Los Alamos and all it stands for, was a national security risk and caused his security clearance to be revoked.

So for Teller to return and face an audience of Oppenheimer worshippers was an occasion that was fraught, to say the least. Damon managed it by first saying that he was there to introduce Teller, and that later in the week, after Teller's scientific remarks, Teller and a violinist he had brought along from Hungary would provide musical entertainment for the audience. "Dr. Teller, as some of you may know," Damon said, "is an extremely accomplished classical pianist, and indeed there may be many in this room who wish he had chosen that path instead of the one that brought him here."

Even Teller roared when he heard that. The ice was broken, and the bones remained intact.

When I arrived in Los Alamos, I asked Damon—because now that I've lived in New Jersey, it meant something to me—where he had gone to high school, since I knew it was somewhere up north. Buh Goat Ta, he responded, and I cracked up. He lived right across from the high school, he said, which placed him within four blocks of where Jim lives, five houses from the place he grew up. I asked Damon if he knew Jim, who is two years younger than we are, and he said of course, his cousin John was in my class. Damon also told me in the course of the evening that his father had been an ice man and delivered ice into New York City, and that by the time he, Damon, was fourteen, he could carry a hundred-pound block of ice with the tongs.

The next morning I called Jim to tell him the news. I was at the breakfast table, and I thought Damon would be there, but he was on the phone. I asked Jim to guess where my buddy the nuclear physicist had gone to high school.

He said, "It wouldn't be Bogota, would it, and his name wouldn't be Damon Giovanielli?" We both laughed, and he continued, "Well, you tell Damon I send my best regards. His father was one of the greatest influences on my life. I still think about him all the time. When I started my wood delivery business twenty years ago, I came home after that first weekend beat to hell, and I sat down and asked myself if I could manage to do this as a way to help make a living for me and my family. Then I said to myself, 'If old man Giovanielli could do it, I can do it,' and every weekend when I'm hauling the logs up those stairs, I think of him and how long he managed to do it, and I keep going."

When Damon finished his phone call, he came in and I told him what Jim had said. He remarked that his father has been dead for thirty years. Glib and smooth as he always is, he had trouble finding any other words, for all the right reasons.

Damon's guided tour of Los Alamos included a stop at the Bradbury Science Museum, where you can put your hand on prototypes of Little Boy and Fat Man, the bombs dropped on Hiroshima and Nagasaki, which gives you an eerie feeling, to say the least, and his pointing out the Episcopal church that he and Ellie go to. When I noted that Episcopalianism was unusual for someone with an Italian surname, he laughed and told me it was worth telling the story of how his family ended up in that church.

In the teens and early twenties of the last century, a number of Italians from the same area in southern Italy settled in Hackensack, just across the GW Bridge from Manhattan. Bogota is directly across the Hackensack River from Hackensack. After a few years, they raised enough money to build a church and purchase a nearby house for a rectory. They went to the bishop in Newark and asked for a priest, and one was soon dispatched.

They hired him a housekeeper, and within a year the priest, the housekeeper, and the church treasury had all gone west, never to be seen again. The Italians went back to the bishop and asked for another priest, but they were told that since the parish had no money, there could be no priest, that the bishop had ordered the church locked so that the holy place could not be improperly used, and that they should disperse themselves among the other parishes in the area. Given that this was still the horse-and-buggy era for many, the reason for the church being built in the first place was that these other parishes required considerable traveling, but the bishop's word was law, and they reluctantly assented.

Several months later came a letter from the disappeared priest, saying that he had heard the news about the bishop and that someday he would pay the money back, which never happened. But he also told them they might have better luck with another bishop in Newark, and he gave them the address. The head of the congregation and two of the other older men hitched up a team and traveled to Newark, where they met with a distinguished-looking man who promised them a priest the next day. Since this was the Wednesday of Holy Week, they were ecstatic.

Sure enough, the priest arrived, broke the lock on the chain that held the doors shut, proceeded inside, and conducted mass, in Italian rather than in Latin. This caused a certain amount of stir, but since the parishioners had no trouble understanding the ceremony, nothing in particular was said at that time. As the priest was greeting his new flock at the front door after the services, a buckboard pulled up, driven by a woman and laden with household effects. "This is my wife," the priest said, and then they realized he was an Episcopalian.

A short colloquy among the elders led the members back inside, where they compared the relative performances of the Roman Catholic and English versions of their faith and decided, especially in light of the services having been conducted in flawless Italian, that the whole congregation would henceforth be Episcopalian, as it remains to this day—St. Anthony's of Padua on Lodi Street.

XXIX HOCKEY GOALIES

BEFORE THE LAST WINTER OLYMPICS, I was lucky enough to get an invitation to a Yale Law School breakfast seminar hosted at a fancy Manhattan law firm—elegant is the word most often associated with its Francophile name—in a conference room located on a floor in the high forties that had great views south from Midtown. The subject was, understandably enough, rules and judges at Olympic games in general, and the host was a senior partner who had been such a judge at four or five previous Olympiads. Not a judge of events, but of eligibility, rules violations, and disqualifications. He was joined on the panel by Mike Richter, an Olympic goalie for the United States and the goalie on the New York Rangers who in 1994 won their first Ranger Stanley Cup since 1937, and Sarah Hughes, the figure-skating gold medalist at the Salt Lake City games. Richter retired and got his degree from Yale, but his professional status prevented him from displaying his talents on the rink designed by Eero Saarinen and known as The Whale for its shape.

If you remember the Salt Lake City games, you probably recall Sarah's unbelievably great performance that won the top spot. She was on fire during her whole program and projected phenomenally right through the TV screen as if she were in the room.

In my former marriage, we had a joke about exceptions to the contract that started with Liam Neeson (but only if he showed up in a tux, inside a stretch limo, with a dozen long-stemmed red roses and Veuve Cliquot on ice for the ride to the Rainbow

Room for dinner and a show). Nicole Kidman joined the list without any qualifications or requirements whatsoever, based on her performance in *To Die For*, and then Sarah, solely based on that incredible exhibition of energy, glamour, and talent. The one wrinkle in Sarah's case was that activation of the exemption necessitated her reaching the age of consent, since she was only sixteen when she won the big one. As of that breakfast, she had done just that in the course of graduating from Yale, despite her father having been Cornell's hockey captain (and, I believe, an Olympian himself).

In the meantime, however, she had been linked in the newspapers with Andrew Giuliani. While in high school, Andrew had been the place kicker on a nationally ranked football team fielded by St. Joseph's in far northern New Jersey, where he presumably lived with his mother. In order to protect the precious leg, he was driven onto the field in a golf cart whenever he attempted a field goal or extra point. Then he went to Duke and managed to get kicked off the golf team by protesting vociferously and rudely when he didn't qualify for one of the six playing positions, making the team only as a backup. Wonder where he got that from, right? But Sarah's pairing with Andrew—long before his father shamed himself publicly as the cartoon lawyer for a cartoon president—had been enough for me to drop her. This would have made a difference if I'd still been married or if there was an ice cube's chance in hell that anything would come of it, but I was glad to stand by my principles. I *had* been glad, that is, because when I entered the room I found a seat not far from and with a good view of HER!

The lawyer host did the introductions and, having been in the stands for her famous performance, lit the torch again with his description of how clear it had been, down to the soles of their feet, to everyone in the arena and watching on TV that she was the winner. He spoke briefly, and Richter a bit longer. Then Sarah took over again and blew away the entire room full of snooty Ivy League graduates of the best law school in the history of the galaxy. To say that she had all of us eating out of her hand, making us each feel as if she were the only other person in the room, is in no way an overstatement. She ruled. She blazed with a pure white flame that was hypnotic. I am still, some time later, unsure if I should just cave in and put her back on the list or insist that she break up with Andrew as a condition. I really want her to dump him in the worst way (both the want and the dump!).

The meeting adjourned to considerable applause, with hand-shakes among the panelists and smiles upon smiles, and the good-sized crowd headed for the elevators and a painful return to ordinary life. Ever alert for bathroom break opportunities, I excused myself and headed for the men's room, where, at the uri-nal for the disabled and the very rare ten-year-old male visitors at this sky temple of the law, I found Mike Richter's son clad in a Rangers' jersey with the name Lundqvist on the back above the number. Henrik Lundqvist is the current goalie for the Rangers.

In addition, the Richter family and I shared a garage with numerous other Upper West Siders, and I had seen the family often, going to or coming home from wherever their weekend retreat might be. I had also seen the family in the audience at the breakfast, so there was no doubt about who this young man was. As I stood next to him, I said the first thing that came into my head, which was "You don't look much like a Lundqvist!" He turned his head my way and gave me a grin so adorable I thought maybe he was related to Sarah Hughes. Then again, his mom is totally cute and Mike has a nice leprechaun look about him as well, so I guess the cuteness was all home grown. We then turned to the basins to wash our hands, and I got exactly what I had been hoping for. Like a true hockey player, young Mr. Richter dried both sides of his hands thoroughly on the front of his jersey, smiled at me again, and headed out to join his family.

XXX HELL ON A HOT NIGHT

MY SON IS MARRIED to a full-blooded Navajo woman who is deeply involved in tribal and environmental matters, as are her parents. His two daughters have Native American names, Tohaana (Guardian of the Waters) and Alowaan (Song). He came into being, and remains, the son of two New York City lawyers, one who practiced finance law for a large Wall Street firm, where they met, and the other associated with Columbia University, where his mom spent more than half of her career. So he made sure both his daughters' names had a Triple A rating, if you look back to earlier in this paragraph. I was the only one who picked up on it, but he confirmed my hypothesis. This is, however, the lead-in to a Woody Allen story, so I've got to cut to the chase and segue to the name Bayard Chapin.

Bayard has a two-million-dollar name. He worked for me and other partners at a law firm that included the name of a man who had been secretary of war for both Presidents Roosevelt. Felix Frankfurter, the notable Supreme Court Justice and Harvard Law School professor, was the first Jewish lawyer there, which would have been back in the first term of Woodrow Wilson as president, if you can believe that. I enjoyed and appreciated the unusual and distinguished place in many ways, without ever feeling thoroughly embraced.

The name Bayard shows up a lot around Manhattan, including on a street now part of Chinatown and on a building on Bleecker Street that is the only work in NYC done by the great nineteenth-century architect Louis Sullivan, appropriately named the Bayard Building. The Bayard family are descendants of Alexis Irénée du Pont, the founder of the DuPont enterprise. A number of U.S. senators, governors, and lieutenant governors, as well as board members of that company, are closely related to the Bayard of whom I speak here. A major street in Princeton also bears that name.

And then there is Miss Chapin's School, still near Gracie Mansion, where the mayors lived before Bloomberg, who bunked with his longtime girlfriend in the house next to the one his ex-wife and daughters lived in. Miss Chapin made a name for herself in the early '20s at the Fifth Avenue girls' school where she became principal, then struck out for mayoral domain and proprietorship near the East River. To show you what she was made of, she insisted on buying the air rights of the surrounding properties, so her school would always have good light and an estuarial sea breeze. Her girls (or at least the school's girls) included Jackie O and Stockard Channing, plus all the granddaughters of the Havemeyer family, who founded American Sugar in 1807 (the factory being located just on the Brooklyn side of the East River) and somewhat less than two hundred years later gave hundreds of millions of dollars of French Impressionist paintings to the Metropolitan Museum of Art. After that donation, they sold off hundreds of millions of dollars more at Sotheby's or Christie's, while watching the auction from behind a large, one-way mirror, sipping champagne and nibbling on foie gras and raspberries.

Okay, maybe Bayard's name was a five-million-dollar moniker. A fine guy who had more to him than his high net worth of relatives and ancestors, he was a good worker and a reliable team member. When he got engaged to be married at the very appropriate age of just under thirty, my wife and I were on the invitation list for the celebration of that event. His wife-to-be was herself well-credentialed and lovely in every way, which I saw for myself when I arrived at the party, at the Cosmopolitan Club, between Park and Lexington and comfortably close to Bloomingdale's.

I had done my homework the day before. Since I had never heard of this club, but knowing Bayard as I did—and considering the various glittery names—I wanted to be prepared and aware of the nature of the venue and the scene I was about to witness. Originally named the Cosmos Club, and situated on East 33rd Street in the Gibson Building (as in "Gibson Girls"), it was founded in 1909 by governesses, but, once their employers took it over, it assumed the more dignified and reserved name it now bears. It also left the neighborhood of Macy's and Gimbel's, and the all too common Empire State Building, moving up closer to Bloomingdale's and the beginning blocks of the prime Upper East Side residential sector.

Among many distinguished members were early suffragettes, other social activists, and household names such as Abby Aldrich Rockefeller (Nelson and David's mother). It is irresistible at this point not to mention that when the original, ultimately tragic World Trade Center was built, it was done to get Nelson the Republican nomination for president by showing he could win by a large margin in New York State, running for governor. To accomplish this, he and his brother determined to secure the support of the building trade unions in the city by erecting those two skyscrapers. Nelson got the legislation through to create the proper public authorities for condemnation of what was on the site at the time, and David, as the head of Chase Manhattan Bank, provided the financing, so the buildings were forever known by union members and certain financial insiders as Nelson and David, with a knowing guffaw often accompanying the phrase. That story ends with Barry Goldwater. The consolation prize was provided by Gerald Ford, who had to supplant both Agnew and then Nixon to pull it off by making Nelson his Number Two.

Woody Allen, eager to take his place on this stage, just elbowed me to redirect myself from that digression, with only one item to be addressed on the subject of the club. It is as gorgeous as you might imagine, with a fine garden in the back. Since the celebration was being held a bit of the way into summer, the place had a kind of white picket fence–ish feeling on the main floor, where the party was in full swing when I arrived. Eleanor Roosevelt, Pearl Buck, Willa Cather, Marian Anderson, Ellen Glasgow, and Custer's widow had once been members of the club as well.

Woody's role, without further ado, involved Bayard's fiancée. She had been his personal executive assistant for a number of years, right out of Finch College (formerly on Upper Park Avenue), from which Tricia Nixon graduated, and where, once a week in season—as I learned from a friend who was on the faculty there—lobster salad was the dish of the day. I knew none of this at the time of the party, since my relationship with Bayard was essentially professional. This was a mere few months after Woody's emergence as a figure of controversy for having "liberated" the young adoptive daughter of his partner, Mia Farrow.

I was working down at Battery Park, with a nice view of the Statue of Liberty, and it was quite a warm mid-July day, so my trip up, while earlier than usual, occurred as rush hour hit its first swell. The only nearby subway went up the West Side, not the East, and you had to either walk eight blocks crosstown underground or take a bus through Central Park at 66th to get to the club. All this is only to say that I was half an hour late. When I phoned my wife, already at the party, she said she'd meet me at the front door, since the place was packed and she could use some air. I arrived, and we did our usual quick huggy-kissy thing. As we separated, she grabbed me by the shoulders and announced, "Guess who's here?" I threw out a few random guesses, like Hillary, Caroline K, or Mandy Patinkin, a favorite actor and vocalist.

"No!" she burst out, wiping perspiration from her face and neck. "Soon-Yi! And Woody!" Then she grabbed my arm, and we set sail to see them. As we crossed the threshold, she leaned toward me and half-whispered through a giggle, "He looks like hell on a hot night!" Not seeing Bayard or knowing his intended, we bee-lined for the largest group on the dance floor and were rewarded by the spectacle. Soon-Yi stood tall, and the sweat flowed over her thinly and smoothly, almost as if it didn't exist to her, but only in the eyes of her beholders. The other Man of the Hour, her consort, hewed closely to my wife's description. If you saw the great documentary *Wild Man Blues*, about Woody's jazz tour of Europe accompanied by her, you may recall that she was extremely self-assured, ordering him and appropriate others around in a firm, clear voice sprinkled with youthful laughter. The recent scandal, the heat, the likelihood that he really didn't want to be there—she had probably insisted on going, to show off, and to participate fully in her new role—combined to make him look like a wet mop after a rugged evening's session on the terrazzo entry hall floor of a Newport mansion. A few moments of that scene sufficed, so we turned to seek relief from a passing waiter bearing champagne, and his sidekick with canapés and hors d'oeuvres. We gladly loaded up as much as our little plates could handle, then located the evening's other happy couple and their families and toasted their good fortune and future lives together.

Angelo Dundee, the wise and resourceful trainer of Muhammad Ali—who also helped fifteen other world champions achieve their goal—provided the winning strategy for Ali's great comeback win against then-champion George Foreman, known as "The Rumble in the Jungle," by sneaking into Foreman's training camp and watching, from a hidden vantage point, Foreman working out with his sparring partners. Dundee noted that Foreman kept his feet a bit too close together to be able to quick-step toward and away from his adversary. He had clearly taken dancing lessons or had similar instruction, since his moves were slick and comfortable. What Dundee extracted from seeing this was that the stance left Foreman poorly equipped to withstand a good solid shot to the body, followed by another of the same. Dundee reasoned that two such blows could cause Foreman to lose his balance, possibly slip trying to keep from falling, and leave himself wide open for a rifle shot to the kisser. He knew that Foreman expected Ali to float like a butterfly—dance and stick, dance and stick—before trying to sting like a bee. Foreman didn't figure that Ali would wade in throwing leather-like blows from the Hammer of Thor.

So he and Ali worked on hammering until it became second nature. Since the spectacle was being held in the Congo, it was certainly a hot night, and the strategy worked to perfection, making Ali again "The Greatest" in every respect. When Dundee was interviewed, sometime after the fight, he staked his claim to a share of the credit for the upset victory, using the deathless phrase only a Philadelphia Eye-talian could craft—"Because when I see things with my eyes, I See Things." Having been where I was, and done what I did, I also can make that claim, and I will tell anybody standing still long enough to hear me out that it was something to see, make no mistake about that.

I went down to Bayard's office the following day and enthusiastically thanked him. I had learned something worth knowing in a general sense, which was that neither Woody Allen nor I was invited to the actual wedding festivities, and my whole conversation with Bayard addressed Woody and Soon-Yi, and nothing more.

XXXI IVY LEAGUE CONFIDENTIAL

MY SON'S FAVORITE New York neighborhood restaurant, aside from Barney Greengrass, The Sturgeon King, at 86th and Amsterdam Avenue, was a small Italian place at about 93rd and Amsterdam. I don't remember the name, maybe Gargiulo's, because they didn't take reservations or credit cards, but the food, service, and ambiance were all first-rate. So when we met for dinner, before he graduated from high school and during his college years, it more or less went without saying that we would go there.

Two equal-sized rooms held the tables, which totaled about two dozen tables for two or four, and two round ones for six or so in the bay windows up front. From window seats, we could wave to those lined up outside, who frequently included friends of his or mine or both. The acoustics were excellent, so conversations could be had, and orders would be understood the first time around rather than when the wrong dish or dishes arrived too late to do much about. This was before the Deluge of iPhones, so the place was relaxed and congenial. Flip phones had emerged by then, but they did not constitute the menace presented by their successors.

The restaurant had a set menu, though it was honored more in the breach than in the observance. There were five or six special dishes, along with several appetizers, which differed every day and were recited by the waiter or waitress who served you. Early on in our visits, we fell under the sway of a waiter named Mike, like me. When I grew up, far from New York City, my parents had an LP they played at all their parties called *Manhattan Tower*, which had been performed as a one-act play on some '50s network TV, with music orchestrated by Nelson Riddle, the great composer and arranger for many stars of that era. It involved an idealized apartment building that had a cocktail lounge and restaurant on its top floor. I mention this record because it featured a song and skit called "Noah," which started with the customers/tenants calling out "Noah! Where is Noah?" when the cocktail hour came around. The intro referred to him as "A wonderful waiter named Noah." Mike must have been his son or nephew, because he was very literate, and a truly delightful person to deal with and be served by.

Mike was, of course, a playwright first, with a new baby son whose name was the same as my son's, so we hit it off right away and always waited until a table was free in his area before going in to eat. Catching up with Mike about his family and his other work was always a treat, but the best part of all was to hear him recite the specials in his distinctive manner, in medias res: "And for pasta—for pasta we have rigatoni with sweet and hot Italian sausage in red sauce with fennel and thyme, linguine with white clam sauce, Manila clams, the small tender ones, vegetable lasagna with broccoli rabe, and tortellini in brown butter sauce with sage and grated parmagiano—pasta."

For each category of the specials, he would introduce and end with the category's name. It must have been a mnemonic he developed—he was also an actor in real life—but until we called it to his attention, he was completely unaware of having incorporated that into his act. Sometimes when we were waiting for a table or making a dinner date on the phone, one of us would spontaneously break into a Mike imitation with a heartfelt chuckle. He also had a reliable set of recommendations, so we never went wrong, which was just another reason that coming back was as automatic as the old NFL PATs from twelve yards out. Since everyone these days communicates essentially in acronyms and thinks in algorithms, I feel a constant pressure not to write in what now seems like old English, the language I learned when I was young, or not to try making things deliberately unintelligible for the reader.

One particular evening, as we were halfway through dinner, two early-thirtyish couples came in and took the round table in front of our section, one of them accompanied by a stroller that resembled a Spanish galleon that should have been part of the Armada. The mushrooming of strollers is another sign of this age we are in, and parallels the mushroom cloud of newspaper, magazine, and blog writers enabled by supersonic keyboards and computers that allow them to disgorge 10,000 words, where 2,500 had previously been adequate for any subject or task.

As the others took their seats, the mom in the group pulled a variety of items out of the cornucopia that protruded from the vehicle's back—this, of course, after seating the two- or three-year-old lad in the restaurant's high chair and placing three or four small items on the chair's tray.

Amazingly enough, that pouch had still more wonders to divulge. We saw that after she had taken her seat and whispered what must have been a drink order to her husband, she then got up to retrieve from the floor the items she had just placed on the child's tray, which she dropped back into the pouch as she thrust her hands into its nether regions.

Now, this is the Upper West Side of the Independent Republic of the West Side of Manhattan. So everyone speaks seven languages, has four degrees from institutions of higher learning, and has either climbed the highest mountain in each of the fifty states or taken a year off to snorkel, helping to restore as much of the coral reefs as possible (which, seriously, do need that and more, or else 85 percent of the fish in the world will die not too long from now). Also, their homes or offices are decorated not with diplomas, citations, or letters of commendation, but rather with original art made by close friends and classmates, or purchased from galleries run by people of that ilk. We know who we are, and we don't much care who also knows it.

As the first in my family to attend college, I was lucky enough to go to a very fine Ivy League institution, courtesy of a scholarship, jobs, and some relatively small loans, since the costs then were microscopic compared to those of today, even if you don't count the bribes now in fashion—or just recently out of fashion. My son, not just to piss me off but irrespective of that factor, attended a competing university and enjoyed it. But he left after three years, to save the world from climate change and all that comes with it. I told everyone that he had left because, after three years, he had learned all they had in New Haven to teach. This comment satisfied the eternal thirst for revenge, but we are both relaxed about it, and we agree on vastly more than we differ on.

It is worth noting that the placement director at his high school also attended Yale (so much for trust and even-handedness), so that of the top fifteen boys in that class of fifty, eleven went to Yale, which shows you why it may be fair to say that George W, by staying the full four years, might likely have learned less than if he'd left sooner. Sorry, that just popped out.

At this moment, the mom unearths a Lucite object about the size of a peewee league soccer ball. It has an icosahedral shape, like a basketball's skeleton, with braided segments composed of the colors of the rainbow! Even tiny hands can easily manipulate it, turning it in different directions, putting a little fist inside the frame and pulling it out again. The boy thus becomes a miniature master of the universe and all he surveys, at the earliest possible age. As my son and I witness this unveiling and the child's complete absorption, we turn to each other and say, in the exact same instant, "Kid's goin' to Hahvahd," and laugh. I then suggest that the baby probably already knew how to say "*res ipsa loquitur*," as well as what it meant, so we have another laugh and call on Mike for the check—leaving, of course in cash, a generous tip by anyone's standards.

XXXII THINKING OUTSIDE THE BOX

ONE OF MY BEST FRIENDS is a thoroughgoing contrarian with a quicksilver mind. Jewish, born and raised on the Upper West Side with a doctor as a father, he became a doctor and then realized he'd done so largely to please his father. He promptly quit medicine, turned to law school, and, after passing the bar, found his way into Big Pharma. He belongs to the NRA because he loves knowing about weapons, though he shoots only at targets. Finally, he thinks everything is funny, or perhaps he has a way of finding everything to be, at bottom, funny, often in highly original ways. At our monthly Chinese-lunch group, during one of NYC's recurrent real estate booms, one of us challenged the group to name any place where prices weren't rocketing upward. Roger, with a semi-second's hesitation, said, "Ramallah." If you don't know, that's a Palestinian city in the middle of the West Bank. Is that funny or what?

His continually off-beat analytical methods led him, fairly early in his career, to come up with a solution to a product problem that threatened to bankrupt his very large employer. The solution was like the purloined letter in the Poe story—it was sitting right in front of everyone, but too close to home for anyone but Roger to see. In fairly short order, he became "the pro from Dover," like Mr. Wolf in *Pulp Fiction*, who is called in to solve unsolvable problems. For the latter half of his career, he had no title and no reporting lines in the company's org chart, because he worked only for the CEO, as an employee without portfolio.

A company as large as his employer always provided snafus of magnitude to hand over to him, along with possession of the CEO's proxy.

This unusual arrangement was based on two principles. First—a rarity in corporate America—someone who did not have a big title, big office, or big ego got paid a very handsome sum for solving problems no one else could solve, which was a good quality to have, but generally underappreciated. Second, since he had no authority other than the kind conferred on a case-by-case basis, his compensation was exempt from the SEC requirements for disclosure to shareholders in annual reports and proxy statements. This meant that none of the other officers had any idea how well he was being paid, so he didn't become the target of a hatchet job or character assassination. He could, however, relish, year in and year out, both the amount he made and the fact that no one other than the boss knew about it!

However, his finest hour, in the opinion of many of his friends, was outside the corporate ambit: as president of the board of his co-op in the high 60s on Third Avenue. Co-op president is often a job avoided at all costs—one chairman of my own co-op actually arranged for his firm to transfer him to London so he could get out of the position. The other side of the coin appears in the form of someone who hasn't risen very high up the corporate or professional ladder, and uses this post to satisfy his need for power. Negotiating contracts with vendors, getting special perks and services from the staff, and (in the worst cases) dipping his pen in the company's checking account—that is, embezzling from his neighbors and friends—seems to plug that hole in his desolate interior.

Roger's talent for problem solving and seeing things others couldn't made him the go-to guy at home as well as at work. Despite his untoward political leanings, Roger had an active social conscience and enjoyed helping others. So he was elected, once he'd said yes, year after year.

Accordingly, he received a phone call at about nine o'clock on a Saturday morning while sitting at his desk and going over some building reports and financial materials.

"Mr. Goldstein," a woman's nervous voice said, "this is Mrs. Meyer in 3B, apartment 3B." Then silence.

"Yes, Mrs. Meyer, how are you today?" Roger responded.

"Terrible, Mr. Goldstein, just terrible. And terrified. I am scared to death, and I need you to do something about it right away. Right now."

Roger affected deep concern, sorrow at learning of her plight, and a willingness to help however he could. His sympathy unleashed from the woman a torrent of words in an increasingly agitated and confused manner. The essence of the situation involved a few things he knew about, and others that were brand-new to him. Yes, he was aware that the tenant in 3A, the apartment next to Mrs. Meyer, was known to everyone but the police to be a drug addict and small-time dealer, and that the man's live-in girlfriend was also an addict. The only previous issues with them, though, entailed playing music too loud and occasionally being a bit late with their maintenance payments. Neither of those problems was unique in the building, so the low-level annoyance had been consistently overlooked in the name of peace in the valley.

No, he had not read the newspapers or looked at the morning news on TV. Oh, really, that was interesting. Would she please repeat it. She definitely would. Two nights ago, the couple had apparently waited until after midnight to make a foray into the upstairs unit of the antiques store that had occupied a building three blocks up for decades. The couple were short on funds—desperately short, one might say—and in their drug-addled dementia had decided that the old man who owned the shop must have some money or pawnable items (preferably money) secreted upstairs. Old and weak as he was, it should be a simple matter to surprise him in his bed, threaten him with bodily harm, and cause him to disclose the whereabouts of his hoard, thus enabling them to purchase the chemical necessaries that were at the heart of their quest.

So they did as they planned, tying him down on his bed and then, after gagging him, searing the soles of his feet with the flames of a small gas torch of the sort used to caramelize sugar in the course of preparing crème brûlée. He was tougher than they had expected, so they pulled down his pajama tops and applied the flame to his gonads. This produced not only hair-raising screams but also a fatal heart attack. No one knew how long the old man had held out, but attempts at resuscitation failed completely.

At this point, the tenant in 3A had apparently thought and acted quickly. He realized that there was no bringing the antique dealer back, and only one other witness to the crime. So he picked up the knife they had used to subdue their victim and promptly stabbed his girlfriend in the heart, rendering her beyond rescue. He did a quick and clumsy job of cutting the antiques dealer loose, putting the girlfriend's body on top of the old man's and placing the knife in both their hands, then skedaddled back home.

The police found him there, well before noon the following day, having had no trouble attaching the address on the woman's driver's license to her likely abode, with the bonus of finding the tenant himself on his couch with an empty bottle of bourbon and a generally catatonic mien. So he had been arraigned and sequestered at Rikers Island, and the entire city's media was now in full cry on the subject of the foul deed or deeds right out of *Crime and Punishment*.

"So," Mrs. Meyer continued, "I want him evicted right now. I won't be able to sleep or hardly even breathe, trying to sleep with my bedroom wall right up against his. You have to help me, Mr. Goldstein! It's your responsibility."

Roger drew a deep breath, exhaled slowly, and took a gulp of his by then rapidly cooling coffee. "Well, Mrs. Meyer, criminal law is by no means a specialty of mine, but I did take several courses in that area, as we were all required to do. I also did rather well in the real estate area of the curriculum. So to be honest with you, you must know that your neighbor has a proprietary lease on his apartment—as all of us do—and that there are limited causes permitted to justify eviction. Being arrested is not one of them, in this building or, I believe, in any other co-op or condominium in the entire city. You might remember that criminal and civil law are two separate legal realms, which gives rise to the criminal code on the one hand and the civil code on the other."

"But he did it. He killed them both, and everyone knows it. What if he's let out on bail and comes back in? I think even seeing him in the hall or the mail room would give me a fatal heart attack right on the spot. Please, Mr. Goldstein, please."

"Mrs. Meyer, I would like more than anything to solve this problem for you, but several things stand in the way. Everybody may know it, but no one has determined as a matter of law that he did it. Like everyone, he is entitled to a trial before a jury and to present whatever defense he can come up with. Don't forget the presumption of innocence that every criminal defendant is entitled to. It can only be overturned in the time-honored way I just went over with you.

"Plus, I need to add, in a case like this, as you have recounted it to me, the benefit of bail has an exclusion, 'where the act is heinous and the evidence is strong,' which sounds like you should feel well protected."

"Oh, Mr. Goldstein, I'm so disappointed in you. Is that the best you can do for me? I'm an old widow, and I have no one to protect me. I'm shaking as I talk to you. I can hardly hold the telephone. This is horrible. Please, please, please."

Roger leaned back, crossed his leg, and scratched his ankle, which had on many previous occasions spurred him past the real world into an area something like *The Twilight Zone*, where entirely different rules applied and solutions no one would regard as anything but crazy turned out to have superior applicability and more force than the humdrum, everyday stuff could ever bring to bear.

"Mrs. Meyer, let me try this out on you. I just had a brainstorm. Here is something I can do that I think will solve your problem—which I recognize is a problem for all of us here in the building, come to think of it. I will locate our super and discuss the matter with him. I'm sure he must be, as you are and apparently everyone but me is, familiar with this horrible situation. He has the master key to all of the apartments. We will go into 3A and examine the premises. And if his floor is not, as required by our proprietary lease, 75 percent carpeted, his butt is out of here, and pronto!" Then, to cut short the inevitable and most likely interminable expressions of thanks, relief, and enshrinement in the Co-Op Chairmen's Hall of Fame, he told her he had to get on with his mission, hung up, and went back to reviewing the building reports and financial statements, confident that, as proved to be the case, he would not hear from her again.

XXXIII FLYING BLIND

A DEAR FRIEND OF MINE who majored in math and lettered in wrestling during college—math because "I hate it, so that was the only way I could think of to learn it"—naturally enough got into the world of publishing. This development was due to the fact that he acquired computer skills via the math when almost no one had them. After working as a consultant, he hooked on with a major publisher of books, regular ones and school textbooks, located near the United Nations on the top floor of an early Depression–era high-rise office building, which was tall for that era, although now not so much.

The firm had a very reputable name and was successful with both fiction and nonfiction, then sold through independent bookstores and chains. Its offices were on the setback floor, twenty stories up, and two others above it. The setback left an area that could be accessed through several doors and then you might lean over the four-foot-high wall, to view Second Avenue traffic and drop ashes, but not cigarettes. No eating was permitted there, and everyone went out to lunch, as we all did in the days before company cafeterias demanded patronage and no one except executives could leave the premises.

This is Carl's story. Like all the stories in this compendium, it's true, vouched for by his former partner, who is a direct descendant of John, John Quincy, Henry, and Francis P. Adams, not to mention Abigail, so how's that for veracity in capital letters?

The firm (and, many would say, our entire country) hit a rough patch somewhere back in the Reagan/Herbert Walker

Bush era, which also featured Jimmy Swaggart and Pat Robertson—the dawn of big-time TV evangelism that mobilized those previously happy just to pray and do church suppers. But enough on that subject. Let's get to the meat.

Essentially, the school-textbook realm became another theater of holy war, purgation, and excommunication, although not in the Catholic sense. Textbooks that referred to many elements of modern science, as well as a great deal of the version of our Civil War propagated for more than a century by the winning side, were found to be heretical and ungodly, and mercilessly excised from the curriculum by being endlessly boiled in holy oil until no one could call those manifestations and "claims" anything but "Red." So they were deleted forthwith.

Some may find it odd that the same clientele were the primary drivers of "Red Scares," from the Palmer Raids of the Wilson administration to Senator Joseph McCarthy's fictitious list of 139 card-carrying Communists in the State Department. Red, however, is just a color, and everyone knows it but the bull.

To put it briefly, this publisher's textbooks on many subjects had been the gold standard in primary and secondary education for decades. They had been updated regularly and meticulously edited by professionals in their field, almost all with PhDs. But, as we're aware, it's not what you know, it's who you know, and all politics is local. And it's not called the Bible Belt for nothing—belt being a tool of corporal punishment not mentioned in that text, but generally agreed to be implied and rarely spared.

So that part of the publisher's business went in the tank. As the former spokesman for two governors of New York once described his job, "You have to be prepared every day to go into the tank for the bigwig who signs your paycheck, and sometimes there's water there, but mostly it's concrete, and you're off the high board when you jump." That was the tank currently in operation, so reduction in staff became a fact among the group of employees who over the years had come to believe there was something like tenure in publishing. Nowadays, there's not really much tenure even in academia, but this was way back when, in what some may argue was the end of a brief golden age.

The fiction side of the business continued to do reasonably well, with its hits and misses. The venture was the next thing to an old-style family operation, with a father figure who had his grasp on everything—his imprint, as it were. He walked the floors and took an interest in all aspects of the firm's activities.

One day, he received an agitated call from an author whose first novel had been published not long before, to relatively positive reviews in the literary press, such as *Kirkus* and other journals mostly read by librarians, academicians, publishers, and booksellers. The firm and the author had found encouragement and hope in what they read, despite not making the *Times*, the *Journal*, or the *Post* (Washington, that is, which did have a well-respected critic who even won a Pulitzer).

The call came in just before noon, a time when, before cell phones, it was amazing that the Manhattan lines didn't melt down because so many people—desperate to complete enough in the morning to justify a two-hour lunch—speed-dialed various numbers into their instruments so they could dump some project or problem on someone else's lap or desk. The agitation was clear in the caller's voice, and so, soon, was the reason.

In very short order, the publisher was given to understand that, through an internal miscommunication, a directive to remove an obsolete Greek-English dictionary from the warehouse and send it to the pulping mill, where it would be converted to fresh newsprint, had caused that fate instead to befall the caller's precious debut novel. Background noise made hearing what the man was saying difficult, not to mention that he was screaming in anger and pain. The publisher shouted over him—he was used to dominating any conversation he was part of, and had a full bag of tricks always ready for deployment. Questions were always good that way. He asked the caller what all that noise was, and how he'd gotten the news and was sure it was true.

"I'm at Teterboro Airport, you creature from hell," the man

bellowed. "I'm at the phone booth by the door to the runway, and I'm about to get into my plane. I'm a licensed pilot and I'm coming to take you out, you maggot-eating turd!

"And how I know about this freaking disaster is that I got the bill for the pulping job from your accounting department, that's how. I have to say you're very efficient when you ruin some-body's whole goddamn life, you son of a syphilitic whore! We'll both be toast in half an hour at most, ha ha ha!"

The publisher knew the author personally, as he did all his writers other than the ones who did the textbooks—those were his employees, which was a different category entirely. He and the author had gone through many wrangles during the prepa-ration of the novel. Even the contract negotiation, which was usually pro forma for a new author, had arduously meandered, over an unusually long period of time, to its signing.

Teterboro was less than fifteen or twenty minutes by air from where he stood at his desk, even allowing for runway delays, so there was no time to lose. His office was on the highest of the three floors, and he dashed frenetically around each floor, tak-ing the stairs two steps at a time, to warn and evacuate his em-ployees. But it was lunch hour, and almost everyone was gone. Even the receptionist had put all the incoming lines on busy. Some years earlier she had suddenly threatened to quit over not being permitted to lunch with her coworkers. Since she was his primary source of inside scoop on the work force, he had bought into her viewpoint without any difficulty.

Only on the lowest floor did he encounter even a single oc-cupant, Mrs. Perkins, whose diplomas contended on the walls with maps of the United States and the world. She was in charge of geography, which was undergoing (then and since) enormous border and name changes. She always worked through lunch and refused to delegate any of her tasks, both for perfectionist reasons and for fear of being supplanted by younger "Greeks bearing diplomas," as she referred to that threat among her clos-est confidants.

The publisher thrust her door open, causing her to actually jump out of her chair and advance toward him in as threatening a manner as a sixty-five-year-old woman of five foot three who weighs 125 pounds could bring to bear.

"Mrs. Perkins," he shouted, "you have to get out of here in no more than ten minutes." He waved his hands toward the elevators in the middle of the building for emphasis.

"Mr. Jovanovich," she shouted back, "that's not fair. You gave Mr. Scott in history sixty days to pack up and go. What about that?"

XXXIV WORKING THE POLLS

IT IS A LITTLE-KNOWN FACT that some of the greatest fun to be enjoyed in public in the Garden State of New Jersey is to work at the polls. It pays $200 for a twelve-hour day, but that includes an hour or so for lunch. You don't have to dress up, many find it one of the few opportunities within the state that doesn't cost you money, and you learn a lot about the system and your neighbors. Plus, most of the time you get to work near your home, because New Jersey has almost as many polling places as dwellings.

When Chris Christie was running for reelection as governor, he arranged to hold the Republican primary on a different day than the Democratic one, so that the media could not compare his race with Cory Booker's first run for senator. The issue was a matter of public safety (like national security but on a statewide basis) because it meant that the people of New Jersey would be protected from the knowledge that their governor was so incredibly less popular than a fledgling black mayor of Newark. This factoid was obvious to anyone who bothered to compare the numbers, gross or percentage-wise, but since the two dates were more than a month apart, that comparison was too much physical and mental effort for more than 90 percent of the registered voters, so the secret remained as secure as it possibly could be.

Even more striking was that the additional election date only cost taxpayers $25 million—don't forget all the polling places, with officials galore and at least three or four part-time poll workers at $200 a pop. It also killed the other historic benefit of poll working. Previously, there were never more than two elections in a year, one primary and one general, leading to a sum of $400 per poll worker. But with the third election, the total passed the threshold for issuing an IRS Form 1099, which lets you, the IRS, and, yes, the state of New Jersey, know about the money. So that took a handsome bite out of what had been tax-free, as was clearly appropriate for the manifestly obese head of state. An e-mail went around the staff of the Morris Museum when Christie's son was admitted to Princeton, on whose board of trustees the governor sits ex officio. The local alumni throw an annual party, with soft drinks and other refreshments, for those families whose offspring have been admitted, and the buzz that year related to whether or not Christie would show up. When his appearance was confirmed, someone in charge of refreshments sent a "Reply All" e-mail (by accident or act of god), observing that, if such were true, they were going to need a lot more brownies!

The usual governmental perks also apply, especially during primaries. Like almost all of America, precincts are generally highly skewed toward one party or the other. I worked a mid-June primary in a heavily Republican town where the current governor, the former governor Christie Whitman—whose father made his money because he got the contract to build Rockefeller Center back in the day—and the state GOP chairman all lived. Since it was after Memorial Day, almost everyone was "down the shore," as they love to say over and again. Eleven voters showed up that day, so it was lucky we had a staff of six, which (I was told by a giggling coworker) was the minimum staff required to host a garden party there. Because this low turnout is more or less typical on primary day, the result is that workers take three-hour lunches, sign in, nod at the others and promise to be right back, then show up just before the sign-out sheet is finalized, with a story of the death by heart attack of a favorite King Charles spaniel, Maine Coon cat, or upstairs maid.

After that first gig, I was lucky to get transferred to a polling place in a railroad station that was a ten-minute walk from our townhouse. Thus, I could get up at 5:45 and be just late enough that it wasn't frowned upon. Meanwhile, the heavy lifting of the day—opening the voting machines and setting up the sign-in books—would have been done, along with taping up the standard posters and warnings on the walls, and setting up the tables behind which we would take turns sitting.

I always brought my own coffee, so I could sit down and spell my colleagues after their initial labors, filling in the numbers 1–50 and 51–100 in both the Republican and the Democratic receipt books. A slip from one or the other was handed to each signed-in voter and then, within five seconds, turned over to the poll worker who pulled the curtain closed as the voter stepped into the booth. Then the worker pushed a large pin through the slip so it could join all the other numbered slips on the string for that party in proper numerical order. There was always a rush when the poll opened at eight o'clock, but you had at least an hour before that to finish coffee and the donuts or pastries brought by the senior poll worker at state expense, and to catch up with other workers' news since the previous election date. Early on I discovered the pleasure of seeing neighbors I was friendly with as long as we kept away from politics, and pretending to be unable to find their names in the voting registers. The combination of a nervous laugh and a highly suspicious scrutiny of my face never failed to give me pleasure.

The paragons of our polling place were two ladies in their well-preserved late seventies, Gail and Gloria, both widows and both immediately identifiable as Republicans by their fresh and firm coiffures and their flower-print silk blouses with matching bows knotted neatly at the neck. Each brought supplementary homemade cookies and stacks of magazines from which they scissored out sumptuous-looking recipes and matrimonial advice for their daughters, plus three or four find-the-word puzzle books, as well as quizzes on various subjects, like rivers, anniversary gifts by year, or other general-interest subjects.

Gloria was a retired schoolteacher whose CPA husband had been a shrewd investor during that period when everyone made money in the market by keeping to the Big Board and away from penny stocks. He had died fairly young and left her with over a million dollars, which she put in a savings account because her interest lay not in making more, but only in not losing any. She had taught for more than thirty years and knew about half the voters who came through, or their parents or children, and we got to know a lot about many of them because she was widely beloved—except by the school board, who had forced her to retire ten years earlier for squeezing a sixth grader too firmly on the upper arm, as she recounted at least once every election day.

Gail had come from money and never particularly thought about it, and was one of the few well-off people I've ever met who seemed to have been made cheerful rather than otherwise by the experience. Her cookies were various and well-considered.

I played the token Democrat—hauling out my backlog of *New Yorkers*, alumni mags, and *The Utne Reader*—and enjoyed helping them with their puzzles. Once Gail asked me if I had ever thought about joining Mensa. I sort of shrugged, trying to consider how to respond, when Gloria bailed me out by leaning in and saying, "No, he only belongs to 'Too Snooty for Mensa.'" The subject was closed at that point, once and for all, to everyone's satisfaction.

To become a poll worker, you needed to attend a half-day class at the municipal Board of Election headquarters. Morristown was prosperous and always sprouting new buildings for administrators, although not for schools, despite their being reasonably well-respected, especially considering the town and township together featured seven or eight private schools of long standing and good reputation. Dorothy Parker (whose real name was Rothschild) graduated from one when Woodrow Wilson was president, and her diploma alone secured her admission to Vassar.

The lecturer for the class, a sturdily built man close to six feet tall and wide, always kept things lively. Well-organized take-away reminder booklets—mostly about what not to forget and who to call if you did—and frequent breaks were popular features of the session. But the winner by several lengths was that whenever the lecturer uttered the words "Board of Election," the sound system immediately greeted it with an enormous burst of cheers, applause, and laughter several seconds long, which produced grins from the stage and all of the attendees.

Our polling place served a varied population. One neighbor who had two grown children with Down syndrome always went into the voting booth with them, showing forms that confirmed she was allowed to assist them. We lived near Convent Station, which had a college and a high school sponsored by the Roman Catholic Church. Each election day, two or three buses full of nuns would show up, sign in while clutching the piece of paper from the mother superior instructing them how to employ their independent franchise, enter the booth, and pass into history.

For the election immediately after Hurricane Sandy, our voting sites were merged into the regional firehouse, which still had power. It was the week Obama was reelected, during which Christie was excoriated by his fellow Republicans nonstop for consorting with the enemy, although he did turn that meeting into money for the state. Three precincts were amalgamated into one. I was chosen to sit at the entryway, check off names, and tell voters whether to go right, into the firehouse where the big trucks kept their home; straight back into the trophy room, which held a great many plaques, trophies, and memorabilia relating to a variety of sports; or back and to the left, where the bar, pool table, and TV lounge were concealed. The most fun was to watch people walk down to the point where you turned left or went straight, and wave brightly, asking to be reminded about whether straight or left was their next meaningful decision. This is by no means to say that they didn't have deeper or stronger issues to address, or that left and right are not strongly divisive and confusing notions to contend with.

Since there is always the same ebb and flow to election days, involving work hours, school hours, and when *The View* is on, I was able to learn a great deal about our larger neighborhood, including the facts that there was only one couple named Dilemma (she was a Dem and he was a Rep), that there were a dozen Murphys—four Dems, four Reps, and four Inds—thus confirming that Murphy's law has a demonstrable corollary, and that there are seventeen ways to write the proper name most crisply spelled "wryly."

The last year I served as a poll worker, we were joined by an obese woman of Irish descent, easily in her mid-seventies, who had been displaced from her home "down the shore" by Hurricane Sandy. She now lived across the way from us, in our ninety-six-unit townhouse development near the train station, with one of her daughters. The development consisted overwhelmingly of families and retired people and was 95 percent Caucasian, with the women displaying a wide variety of short haircuts in shades that ranged from snow-white through lilac, heliotrope, and on to a sky blue most famously seen in Doris Day's and Grace Kelly's eyes. People left at dawn and returned after dark, or didn't come out much at any time of the day. The only exceptions involved the children's school buses, which showed up around four o'clock in the afternoon and were always met by parents.

This primary election day was in the late spring, and our neighbor shared with us her experiences during that winter in the wake of a historic snowstorm. The huge storm had led to enormous piles of ice where the walkways had been cleared by shovels and plows. Our coworker had slipped and fallen while taking her late-morning walk up and down the block, then lain, unheard and unnoticed, in the snow and ice tunnel of her family's walkway to the street, for a number of hours.

"I called and cried, but nobody answered, and when I tried to reach my cell phone, I couldn't locate it in my parka or my pants. Finally I just lay there and called out when I thought I heard someone. At last, a dark-skinned young man with short hair came up our passageway. Luckily, he had a cell phone, and he got the fire department to come and rescue me. You know I couldn't stand up on my own, that was for sure.

"So they rescued me and I got back home safe. But he said his name was Donovan, and I've wondered about that for the last several months." She was telling her story in late afternoon during the long lull between school buses and commuters returning from the City. She commanded the floor, as the rest of us waited for the ending or whatever. Eventually, she drew her breath and shared it with us. "So I kept asking myself, how could he be so dark and still be Irish?" Then she slowly reached her right arm up from her new wheelchair, tapped her forefinger against her temple several times, and said, "Oh, I get it. Black mother. So that's what it was!"

XXXV GOOD OLD JOHN

MY FIFTEEN-YEAR-OLD CAR was in the shop because the engine light kept coming on for no reason, which the mechanic attributed to a faulty carbon monoxide sensor triggered by frayed wiring that necessitated taking apart the frammis and the whatsis and several other dohinkeys. So I was using my girlfriend's car, which she treasures like a teddy bear, when I got a call from my ex asking if I could pick her up from the clinic where she was having a procedure that she wasn't allowed to drive home from, although the procedure wasn't a major deal. She had someone to drop her off, she told me, but no ride home.

I said yes, of course, but didn't mention it to my girlfriend for obvious reasons. I also made a lunch date with a friend of mine who lives near my ex, partly as a cover story for why I needed the car. I picked up my ex and took her home, and she invited me in for a beer. We had a nice catch-up chat about my kids, her niece and family, and played with her dachshund for a bit. Then she asked if I wanted another beer. We hadn't seen each other in about a year and had talked only once or twice briefly after a marriage of seventeen years, and my collar was starting to feel tight, so why push your luck, I said to myself. No thanks, I replied, I had to move on. Then we had a civilized hug, she thanked me, we wished each other well, and I was out of there.

Eager as I was to leave the premises, I looked at my cell to check with my friend, who is often late, about his expected arrival time for lunch. To the left of the driveway, at the place where the sidewalk and the drive met, stood a large oak tree that blocked my rear view. As a result, I managed to hit an SUV that was parked across the narrow street at the corner of the opposite driveway. The sound was almost inaudible, a sort of *tick*, from fiberglass caressing other fiberglass. I got out, to find the driver of the other car bending over his fender and pulling out his cell phone.

I had recently rear-ended another SUV at five miles per hour when the driver stopped short in front of me to turn left without signaling while I was changing the radio station. There are three or four songs I cannot bear to hear—"Piano Man," "Michelle," "The Cat's in the Cradle," and "Raindrops Keep Falling on My Head"—and one of those had come on the radio. No one was hurt, but the high bumper of the SUV totally cratered the front end of my fifteen-year-old Lexus sedan, with $4,500 of damage to my car and a minor scratch on hers. The local police had arrived and ticketed me, and I had pled guilty and received an $85 fine and no points, because of my good driving record and the lack of damage to the other party. That's how I acquired the *new* fifteen-year-old car that had the frammis/whatsis problem, which landed me in my girlfriend's car, whose rear bumper in this case now displayed a very minor scratch, although I knew she would notice it.

The other driver pointed out that his fender had sustained a dent about the size of a silver dollar—an apt analogy, as the reader will see. It was also about as deep as a coin that size. I told him this was my girlfriend's car and I didn't want to cause a problem with her insurance, so I would be happy to pay for the damage.

He thanked me and dialed 911, explaining that his was a leased car and he needed to report the incident "just in case, so I don't get stuck with the bill." The police arrived, I showed both my girlfriend's insurance card and my own, and the officer said there was no need to report the accident, especially since we were working it out between the two of us.

A ding, he called it.

At this point, John, who said he was on a business call and whose card stated he was a real estate appraiser, told me that a body shop near his home could do the work, so I said fine. He noted that the car would probably have to be in the shop for a week or so, so he would need a rental car. I expressed surprise about the length of time but assured him I would cover the cost, and would send him a letter laying out all the details, to put him at ease.

I called my friend again, but he was "just about to call to cancel." So I had lunch on my own, the high point of which was that the son of a very nice woman I had dated—after my divorce and sort of before my girlfriend—came and sat next to me at the bar with a friend and didn't recognize me, so we had a nice conversation. His not recognizing me was good, since I had broken things off with his mom politely after meeting my girlfriend. Plus, I had had too much fun before that at a big pool party at his McMansion, including telling his wife some things his mom had told me that I really should have known better than to pass on.

The body shop appraisal came to $3,500, not including the car rental. I was amazed, but a detailed estimate from the shop that accompanied the fax mentioned replacing the fender and front bumper, since it was a unit, and repainting that side of the car so it would all match. So I said okay and took some money out of my IRA.

My girlfriend and I went to England and had a jolly old time. On the flight back, I handed over my credit card to pay for our drinks. My girlfriend told me to use our American Airlines credit card, since we got a 10 percent discount with it. So I pulled out my wallet and used that card instead. Because I was belted in with a full tray right up into my midsection, I put my wallet in the basket on the back of the seat in front of me, to retrieve when we arrived at JFK.

You guessed it. We were almost to Customs when I realized my wallet was missing. The Customs guy dragged me to the American Airlines agent and was insistent that I be helped immediately, but the plane had already been taken to the hangar for maintenance and cleaning. This meant that, after going home around midnight an hour and a half away, we would need to come back the next day in hopes of retrieving my wallet. The savings on the drinks had come to ninety cents.

When we got home and I checked my e-mails, I found a day-old one from John, saying that his car was ready and needed to be picked up on what was now the next day—by three o'clock, because it was a Friday and body shops in New Jersey (which has the highest auto body repair costs in the country) close then and don't open again until Monday at eight. Since no one at the shop knew me, I had to pay in cash or with a credit card. All my credit cards and my ATM card were in my wallet, of course. At about three in the morning, after an hour or so on hold with the airline, I had learned that it had been found with apparently nothing missing.

So we drove back to JFK the next morning and recovered my wallet. I stopped to get the cash for John to cover the $450 for the replacement rental SUV and drove first to his house, to pay him, and then to the body shop. When I went upstairs to the office, four guys were sitting around a table drinking coffee and schmoozing while a young lady manned a bank of computers behind the counter on the other side of the room. I went up to her, told her who I was, and gave her my credit card. One of the men came over—he must have been the boss—and asked her what this was about. "Oh," she said, "it's about that Ford SUV, the one John DiVincenzo brought in. With the messed-up front end." She smiled.

"Who?" he asked.

"You know," she responded with an even bigger smile while pulling the bill out of the printer, "John who lives over on Maple Drive. John DiVincenzo."

"Oh, yeah," he responded. "John. Good old John."

"Yeah," she replied. "Good old John."

"Good old John?" I said to myself. "Good old John?"

Boone Pickens said if you're in a poker game for one round of deals and you don't know who the pigeon is, it's you. No, John was not a real estate appraiser. He slowly patrolled suburban neighborhoods and pulled over just as some chump was backing out of a driveway a little too fast and positioned his car artfully to produce the telltale ding. The SUV wasn't leased, it belonged to the body shop, and John was a procurer, on commission. The cash for the replacement rental car was his off-the-top reward, and he was probably getting a piece of the body shop's plunder as well. For all I knew, my ex had set the whole thing up because she was still pissed off at me about the divorce, and was also getting a piece of the action. The whole thing—the procedure, the beer and playing with the dog, right down to the chaste hug and kiss on the cheek—was right out of Mae West's playbook, although Mae was from Queens, not Jersey. But so was my ex. I looked at the three other guys sitting around the table and drew a deep breath while I considered my situation and my options. Then I thanked the owner and office manager, waved to the other guys, and got the hell out of there.

I don't live in New Jersey anymore. One good old John is rich enough for my blood. I later learned that he had the same name as the Democratic county leader, so maybe he was just moonlighting for the cause.

XXXVI THE BULLY AND THE BURGERS

THE BIGGEST BANKRUPTCY in American law firm history didn't come about by accident. Character, as so often, was at the heart of it, along with greed, of course, but buffoonery didn't lack for a part in the production. During the firm's fortieth-anniversary black-tie dinner on the St. Regis roof, Adrian Leiby—at that time the third senior name partner—started his five minutes of remarks in honor of Randall LeBoeuf by citing as the source of his inspiration a commercial heard while driving in from New Jersey that morning, for Silver Floss Sauerkraut, whose slogan was "You were just a little cabbage from Phelps, New York, but you made it big in the Big Town." Mr. LeBoeuf followed with a half-hour oration—which had been edited down from a full hour by his estimable secretary, Emily Cutler Essex. He told her the next Monday that he wanted to deliver the excised portion (that is, the dull part) at the next monthly partners' or associates' lunch, but that speech somehow never found fruition.

Power is generally apportioned and wielded in an ad hoc manner in any group or organization, as in the way Dick Cheney arranged to head the committee to choose W's vice president, got himself appointed to that post, and then took over the presidency—using the route and rationale laid out in the 25th Amendment but without the rigmarole (the procedures and standards) otherwise laid out therein. He also went to Congress carrying a briefcase that he told the Speaker of the House contained an armed nuclear device, but did not. That, however, is just an example of how he used his power, not how he obtained it.

My favorite example of buffoonery involves how I acquired the trappings of power, although very little of the real thing. One morning, as I was sitting down at my desk, a favorite associate lawyer of mine came in and congratulated me. I asked for what, and he said for being named to the Executive Committee, of course. I had been at the firm for almost twenty years, so the appointment certainly made sense to me, but I asked him how he knew this while I didn't. He told me everybody knew it. The evidence was everywhere, like when limousines gather around the Kremlin and stay there late into the night, then suddenly all become reoccupied and leave when the deed or deeds have been done.

In this case, the math and the biology made it clear. For a long period, we had a one-man, one-vote system. Cameron Mac-Rae, Sr., was the man, and he had the vote. When he retired, the firm had another sumptuous party, this time at River House, on the East River at 55th Street. As an appropriate retirement gift, some clown had purchased a leather desk set—medium-green blotter, pencil cup, box for scissors, ruler, and staples, lidded paper clip container, and matching marble and gold pen and pencil holder, with an engraved gold plate bearing his name and the thanks of the firm.

Cameron was not THE MAN for no reason, and he knew his audience inside out. He paused, thanked the Gift Committee, and observed that his homes in Manhattan, Southampton, and Hobe Sound in Florida already were adequately provided with this type of equipment. He then waved the blotter like a banner on parade, remarking that a beautiful set like this deserved to be properly displayed. This meant, as far as he could see, that he needed to rescind his declaration of retirement and give it another five years or so to see things through. As the saying goes, the silence was deafening, until he told the crowd that it was okay to laugh at his joke. The laughter slowly arrived and kept building for a considerable time, fueled as it especially was by the release of anxiety among the five newly named members of the Executive Committee.

But in any morphological situation, the morphing continues, so in about five years, the committee had not changed, although the firm had. It had grown, both in numbers and in revenues and arguably in profitability. In the normal law firm system, December is the month during which each of thirty partners makes the case behind closed doors to the members of the committee to the effect that he, and occasionally she, is personally responsible for 20 percent of the firm's work and profitability and could get properly compensated for those results elsewhere if, sadly, justice didn't prevail at home. After five years, sixty partners were making the same claim, so something had to be done.

By this time, each member of the Executive Committee was generally known to be involved in one or more extramarital romantic relationships, in or out of the firm. The "Tone at the Top" that allegedly drives the moral and ethical institutional dimension was busily wandering off-key. That excluded the one member who had married his secretary. At a party for the summer associates and a portion of the permanent lawyers in the home of that partner, I discovered that the mistress of another member had spread a dozen of her business cards—she was a stockbroker—on the entry hall table upon arrival. I casually pocketed them to restore the semblance of propriety. But since the couple lunched regularly at the business club where most of the partners ate free, and a few wags were given to sending "complimentary" bottles of wine to their table—complimentary in the sense that both the sender and the recipient were paying for only a small portion of the partnership's cost of the bottle—my gesture only went so far. Therefore the Gathering of the Limousines.

The Executive Committee had five members, one for each major department and one for the DC office. No lawyer worth his or her salt is likely to know the difference between meiosis and mitosis, but that is what the limos accomplished. Each department and the DC office had doubled its number of representatives on the committee, with the newbies all ten years younger than those in situ. Only a considerable time later did the younger crew learn that the older guys continued to hold their own meetings before the "joint" meetings, to determine the agenda of the latter and to decide which issues they would support as a bloc and which ones they would unanimously oppose.

December arrived, with its regular rituals, two in particular: New Partners, and Partnership Compensation for the next year. Once, at the famous Skadden Arps law firm—which became a dominant merger-and-acquisition firm, an enormously lucrative field—the bonus pool was divided entirely among members of the Bonus Committee, leading that period to be known forever after as "The Year of the Pig." We were more subtle, or at least we believed so among ourselves—the committee, that is. For one thing, we had as part of our governance a "Council" (of Counsel, of course). This group of another twenty partners met to learn what the Executive Committee had decided and rubberstamp it, then adjourn for a dinner provided by and in the cafeteria, but with wine.

For the work of the committee to be done properly, it had to be done in secrecy. This meant meeting on Saturdays—since evening sessions would be noted and gossiped about—and starting early so that we were all secreted in the large conference room before any of our Weekend Warriors were likely to arrive and notice the odd combination of heavy hitters assembling. We planned to adjourn by mid- to late afternoon for the same reason and also because we did, after all, have lives to live, families to nurture and other things to do. But in the meantime, millions of dollars were on the table to be spread around.

The agenda at my first meeting on the committee related to partner compensation. Hours upon hours of discussion could be had, especially among good lawyers, about how to format such a process, but we did it as it apparently had always been done, which was to leave the more difficult issues to the end— that is to say, the high end of the comp table. Since there were many more junior or less generously compensated partners, some with equity in the firm and some with fixed salaries, this deliberation consumed a considerable amount of time, in that it involved a general conversation about each person's performance in the year mostly gone by. Over time, this unwritten record would evolve into the basis for horse-trading between departments, larger or smaller increases, and so on.

The discussion was detail oriented, since part of being our kind of lawyer involved meticulous attention to detail. We all knew the story of the partner at another firm who had misread the principal amount of a ship's mortgage by one decimal point and turned the ship owner's hundred-million-dollar debt into a ten-million-dollar one, leaving the lender—and, accordingly, the firm—ninety million dollars short. Something was worked out in that situation, but with enormous pain and effort on all sides. So we dotted our "i's" and curled our "q's" quite carefully and in concert.

Late in the morning we had struggled to get into the upper-middle ranks. Since the results largely involved raises of between five and ten thousand dollars in an expansionary economy, it was reminiscent of the answer to the question of why academic disputes are so contentious and drawn out: because there is so little at stake. But we were also building a case, for the Council and for the discussions with the individuals if challenged, about why Partner X got a $5K larger raise than Partner Y, especially if they worked in the same department. The reasons could be manifold; the idea was to settle on a story and stick to it. We were well along, to the point of our office manager starting to pass around lunch menus from the burger joint downstairs.

At the head of our table sat a man whose department probably accounted for the largest single share of the billings. Our firm had a preeminent position in two major industries, one financial and one industrial, with both involving a good deal of international work—a pretty picture, to be sure. His main stewardship was devoted to an enormous financial institution overseas. The interesting thing about the relationship was that all correspondence with the client, which had many points of contact, was

186 | The Bully and the Burgers

read by all the lawyers who worked with or for that client irrespective of whether they had any involvement with the matter
or issue at hand. Can you hear the cash register ringing with the
results of the billable hours totted up every year by this exercise?
The task was so amorphous that there was no way to determine
the accuracy of the amounts billed, and discounts were always
factored into the annual retainer. But without belaboring the issue, when Boss Tweed said, "I seen my opportunities and I took
'em," he didn't speak only for himself. To add more detail to the
portrait of this department head, those unkindly disposed toward him referred to him as someone who was selling law by the
pound with his hand on the scale. His upbringing and education were distinctly outer borough, although the complete "kit"
(as they say in Australia) of his substantial person was Brooks
Brothers head to heel. You might best describe him as a force of
nature bulgingly enwrapped in a sort of silk purse. Because of
his personality, although in contravention of his ethnicity, he
was known as The Don.

Several years before, we had taken in a "lateral" partner from
one of the top five firms in the City. His elite NYC background,
including the fact that his grandfather—head of an investment
bank—had maintained his own string quartet, while his grand-
mother had been the mistress of a very famous author, led him
first to be expelled from two of our leading schools for the education of our society's and government's leaders, and then to
conduct affairs with the wives of two of the partners in the firm
that had finally decided not to bring him into their own partnership. Too much of a good thing, perhaps? But his credentials
were impeccable, and his talent was at a level we could rarely
compete for. We had no major bank, which was the cornerstone
of practice for all WASP firms, or investment bank, which served
as same for the top Jewish firms. That made us permanently just
below the top tier, which was still a completely lovely place to
hang our hats. We took him in on the strong urging of a senior

member known for producing business, but always in need of someone to do the work once it was landed.

This newish partner had a habit of working with his office door open and his feet on his desk, shoes off, and wearing a set of apparently hand-knit, bulky socks of various earth tones. He was equally insolent to one and all, but his work was beyond reproach and always commanded the respect of clients and the people on the other side of the table. He somehow managed to appear at peace even while he roiled everyone else's waters within the firm.

Some of our earlier discussion at the committee meeting had related to decreases in standing, which were rare but did sometimes happen. One partner was barely permitted to remain with the firm after butchering a deal that involved the construction and financing of a major sports arena. That debacle had led to drawing on our malpractice insurance and been resolved internally by requiring him to take a serious cut in pay but also to cough up his set of four Yankees' season tickets (in the second row between the foul screen and the visitors' dugout), and to never go to a client meeting without his "seeing eye dog," which was our code name for the younger partner assigned to shadow him in all business dealings. His connections with the ownership of the Yankees helped him keep his position, and the tickets helped grow the practice, so all was well that ended well.

But when we came to the case of the guy with the socks and the open door, it appeared that he had made a mortal enemy out of The Don. This was due partly to refusing some work from him as too simple for one of his breeding and skills and partly on account of the socks. Since The Don had sacrificed his own authenticity, trading his Queens accent for a modified Oxford/Cambridge lisp along with white collar and cuffs and gold cufflinks, he could hardly stomach the sight of such reverse snobbery. Something had to give.

Much to our surprise, what The Don laid on the table was the expulsion of the miscreant. At first, he called for his demotion and a reduction in his compensation. But then The Don swiftly withdrew that downgrading as inadequate to the unstated, but allegedly well-known, violations of spoken and unspoken rules we all adhered to without deviation.

The fellow facing ejection was a friend and colleague of mine, and I enjoyed his mild-mannered but unmistakable disrespect for phoniness, as well as his strong intellect and sense of professionalism. As other members around the table hastened to support the big man's initiative, I was amazed at how the bullying process, which began with overstated and generally unjustified complaints, suddenly escalated and then whacked its way into mob rule. The personal dimension explodes on cue from the "leaders," so "cheerleaders" or "lynch mob" is more accurate.

So The Don's raising of the cry brought out the least and the worst from our leadership, and we were slipping rapidly when I raised a point of order, framed as a hypothetical. The best thing about hypotheticals, the cornerstone of legal education, is that they are framed by experts in creating confusion, many professors having spent some time as trial lawyers. They are also mine fields, in which a number of issues and processes are interwoven in the text. The student has a very short time to think about them and provide an answer. The class grows still, either responding by asking *whaat?* or trying to dope out a solution. Youth is optimistic, and the answer arrives, if it does, late in the game—that is, if there is an answer at all.

I called attention to the time of year and to the volatile, unpredictable nature of the sock man's personality. Then I mentioned as casually as possible the recent incident involving an employee of a West Coast airline, a gate agent who had a history of doing things his own way. While very effective in his job, he was insolent and rude to his fellow workers, of whom he held an often-expressed, abysmally low opinion, which made cooperation difficult, tending toward impossible. He had been warned about his behavior but had not reformed, and a hearing to

determine whether grounds for termination existed was sched-
uled at headquarters in Los Angeles. The agent worked in the
Bay Area, which meant that he, the accusers, and several members of the upper echelon up north had to take a special plane to
attend the hearing.

What happened was simple. The special nature of the group
of passengers allowed them to dispense with normal check-in
security. (This incident occurred before 9/11, after which nothing stayed the same.) Aware of this, the agent smuggled a .357
Magnum on board in his briefcase. Soon after takeoff, he apparently pulled it out, blew everyone else on the plane to perdi-
tion, and the plane crashed. Our conference room experienced
a stop-time moment. Everyone but me turned a translucent
white—deathly would be where you would look for the shade
on a color chart—and it felt as if all the air had been suctioned
out of the room.

If you saw a real-life film of the occasion, you would have
thought that a minute or two had been snipped from the reel.
Without any further discussion, the menus from the hamburger
joint started getting passed around the table, and our discussion segued seamlessly into whether the French fries could be re-
lied upon not to show up soggy or limp, and if that uncertainty
then suggested the tomato-and-lettuce side salad as a superior
choice. As to beverages, we were unanimous on diet Cokes with
lemon wedges. In another two minutes, one us suggested that
we call in the office manager to deliver our orders and move
along to the next person on the list, which we did.

No one ever mentioned the incident to me afterward, and
so it slid into one of those cracks in history where events that
never happened are stowed for good. Saving that guy's job
might or might not have been the noblest act I performed in
my thirty-five-year career, but whenever I thought about it, it
always prompted a broad smile, a small yet healthy chuckle, and
an overall feeling of well-being, especially after I left the firm
two years later.

XXXVII TOP GUN SCHOOL SANCTUARY

AFTER LAW SCHOOL, I was lucky enough to get an office mate who was three or five years older than me and whose background differed entirely. Having been brought up as the son of a U.S. Army officer, I had received scholarships and loans (small by today's standards) to land me a position where I had the window side of a two-person office with a direct view of the Statue of Liberty from the forty-eighth floor. Bill, aka Wing Commander Davisch (two syllables, please), had grown up in the hard-scrabble area of Hartford (not West Hartford, he was always eager to correct people). His father worked at Pratt & Whitney on the airline assembly floor, watched Friday night fights from St. Nicholas Arena in Manhattan, and stayed at Clancy's Bar until Bill came to bring him home, starting from the time he was eight. Then he went off to UConn, ten miles away, and lived in a frat house. He graduated, enlisted, went to Officer Candidate School, became an officer and then a navy pilot, did his five years before Vietnam got hot, and made the *Michigan Law Review*. Hence his getting the chair by the door in our office, since I was a Yale Law graduate, I supposed. Luckily, our mutual lower-class upbringing helped us bond. I got the benefit of his five years in the Pacific fleet and provided him with whatever I had gleaned as a High School Harry (not a Peter Prep) crawling through the Ivies.

Our law firm was top-shelf—everyone was Ivy or equivalent, and Michigan certainly qualified. The senior partner had been Governor Al Smith's chief of staff and founded the firm in

October 1929. One thing most people don't realize about the Depression is how little it affected those who had money that was connected with real assets, not Wall Street trading or speculation. This group might have felt pinched, but ultimately they didn't do that badly, and their descendants have fought continually against the New Deal "social safety network" for the last eighty years, fueled by the cash from utilities, oil companies, suppliers of war materiel, vast agricultural and meat-producing and -processing enterprises, and their professional enablers, of which our law firm was certainly one.

Slow down and don't work too hard, Bill's dad had learned and passed on to him from his time on the assembly line. "If you go faster, they ask you to go faster still, so we just look at them like we don't know what they are talking about" was something he had picked up at his father's knee. I, by contrast, was driven to success by an insane set of underachieving parents. Long after my mother died, I ran across a bundle of her grade-school report cards. After the endless hounding she gave me about ever getting anything as low as a B$^+$, I laughed and almost cried when I saw that my worst report card was enormously better than any of hers. My warning to parents is not to try to succeed by forcing your child to live the life you yourself could never pull off. What that meant for Bill and me was that our office became the social center, with Davisch and others trading stories, gossiping, and playing "Executive Waste-Basketball" with a backboard and net mounted on a wastebasket set on the top of a five-foot-high bookcase, into which we tossed neatly formed balls shaped from legal-sized pages. Bill had the franchise on creating those, since he folded neatly and always enjoyed watching others play more than he liked playing himself. Back then, you could smoke in your office, and he had a pipe. Every payday, one of us would go and buy a box of Royal Jamaica coronas and parcel them out one a day until the next payday. Life was simple and even fun.

Bill was fascinated by all the Ivy League traditions he had never encountered and loved to probe about how they arose and were perpetuated. He particularly loved the "Skull and Bones" society rule that if those precise words were uttered in a group containing a Bonesman, that individual was obligated to leave the group as quickly as possible without revealing the reason for his departure. The reason, of course, was to preserve the secrecy of his "Secret Society," although the general view of the non-Eli's in the room was that leaving seemed more like the best way for people to know that you were, for sure, a member. Bill certainly held that view, and it was difficult to argue otherwise.

One day another Eli, not a Bonesman, showed up for afternoon "Chowder and Marching Society," as we dubbed our afternoon coffee break, with a new green tie featuring large roosters. I looked at the tie, looked around at the six of us packed into our small office, and said, "Big Red Cock." That was recognized as a Bones-like utterance, and we all dashed for the door, pushing and shoving and laughing as we spilled out like so many Marx Brothers leaving a stateroom through the porthole.

For some reason, Bill's time in San Diego was his favorite stretch in the Navy. He told the story about being officer of the day when a high-ranking enlisted man—a "lifer"—came to see him for advice about a recent "situation" he'd been involved in, which featured the couple who lived next door in the NCO married-housing section of the vast base. (I once stayed in the Hotel del Coronado on Coronado Island, very near the armed forces bases that dominate the landscape. My room was ground floor and opened onto the beach. I got up one morning and put on my swimsuit, readying for a morning dip, but when I pulled the curtains apart, I saw fifty Navy Seals executing an amphibious landing with ten rafts, and with two carriers and eight helicopters supporting them. I went and had breakfast instead.)

Bill's "lifer" explained that the foursome had done a lot of drinking before and during dinner. Then someone suggested playing strip poker. That in turn led to the idea of wife swapping. As Bill told us, "So the guy looks at me and says, 'I mean, Commander Darisch, it was just like the movies. I'm banging his wife, he's boinking mine (she's Swedish, is why I say it that way), we're grinning at each other like how much fun is this. But then the wine started wearing off and we started looking at each other like, oh my god, what have we done here? So what should I do now? I think it was a wrong move, but I don't really know how to end it gracefully.'"

Bill continued the tale, saying that he'd thought for a second and then recommended dropping by the neighbor's after work or, if he and the neighbor worked together, getting some coffee—either way, making the opportunity to say he'd had a dream about those activities, although he was sure it hadn't actually happened. Wink, wink, nod, nod, and suggesting that should be the final word. "I never heard anything else about it," Bill finished, "so either that suggestion worked, or they liked it too much to cease fire, as it were."

Another of his favorite stories involved the pilot who had to ditch his plane during a training run because he could finally see the fuel gauge and realized he was well short of the amount necessary to return to base. One member of the court of inquiry asked why it had taken so long to notice that fact, and his reply was simple. His route first led west, he said, out into the Pacific, and it was late in the day. Furthermore, the setting sun was right in his eyes, so he couldn't see the gauge accurately until the sun went below the horizon. I think you can figure out how that tribunal concluded, but at least the pilot didn't have to pay for the plane.

Best of all, however, was the wild and merry chase a fellow pilot had led the California Highway Patrol on down the San Diego Freeway at about 115 miles per hour one Friday night after a lively tour of the local gin joints. He sees the "misery lights" go on atop the cruiser and, remembering the medieval concept of "sanctuary," quickly calculates that he can make it back to base before the guy catches up with him. So off he goes, pedal to the metal, and in his sports car he slides neatly under the bar across the lane at the hut manned by the shore patrol at the entry point.

He pulls over thirty feet inside the base, watches the CHP confer with the shore patrol, and then sees the bar go up and the cruiser roll onto the base. At this point, he realizes that the Highway Patrol guy will know he's been drinking, so he reaches under the dashboard, pulls out a full pack of Doublemint gum, unwraps all five sticks, and crams them into his mouth, chewing nineteen to the dozen, as the saying goes. The cop stretches out his hand and says, "License and registration, please, son." He sits there for a moment, rolling the tinfoil from the gum between his thumb and forefinger, and finally puts it into the cop's hand, saying, "Well, officer, I don't happen to have those with me tonight, left them in my flight suit. But I think this silver bullet will give you some idea of who you are dealing with," which ended his flying career.

XXXVIII PERSONAL BEST

"NOT LIKE THAT, not like that, not like that." My father liked to repeat himself three times for emphasis, "to possibly get it through your head," he would say, especially on the golf course after one of my topped balls or wild sliced shots—worm burners or moon probes, as he dubbed them. That chiding was part of his relentless effort to make me into a golfer, or any kind of athlete at all. But particularly a golfer, because he loved the game, even though he didn't shoot much lower than the high eighties, breaking a few putters and denting with his weapons of the moment the sides of wooden rain shelters and toilet facilities around the Army courses in Europe and the lower forty-eight, most notably when his game was in more of an ebb than a flow.

But this wasn't my father saying it. He's dead ten years, eleven this coming September. This threefold repetition was me, regressing under stress, showing that the end of this round, my first real shot at breaking 100, with my son alongside me at the sixteenth tee, was starting to become a race between fatigue and the burden of history.

I had just hit a rocket deep into the bushes on the left of the fairway. All afternoon—between the end-of-the-morning crowd and the beginning of the thrifty twilight-rate players—we'd had clear sailing around the course, but for these last two holes we'd had to wait and watch a very cheerful foursome fire an array of blasts into the trees and the rough, back and forth across the fairway, on and on. Their comedy had shed its charm by now, and I was trying to pass the time by running my tee across the

195

grooves of the club face at a speed most chefs would use to produce hollandaise sauce.

Three more holes, average five shots a hole, and I'm in with a 98. I shot 100 last year, not paying any particular attention but knowing that for me, whose recorded high is 168, it had been an unusually trouble-free round. I gave the game up for many years after the torture of having my father teach me. Whatever relationship we had as much as disappeared when he got me out on the practice range or the course and started telling me things like the trick the old-time golf teachers used—I was thirteen at the time—to make you keep your head down on the shot, which was to tie a string around your ear, attach a large fishhook to the other end, and embed the fishhook in the crotch of your trousers, so if you pulled up, the fishhook would sink into your scrotum or penis. We differed on whether this was funny or not, and the perverse result was that I began to wince every time I pulled up, which was eight times out of ten, without there ever being a real fishhook involved. Everyone agrees that golf is 99 percent between your ears—that is part of how it becomes an addiction and spawns so many jokes—and this was my first look through that window.

The other 99 percent is in the physics: the objective reality of weight and torque and distance, and the math and the exactitude and the large opportunity for error. My dad had no patience to spare, and his career of turning boys into men for Uncle Sam made him feel comfortable using nicknames like bozo and klutzie as he pointed out my faults and shortcomings, in golf and otherwise. He may have thought he was being jocular and affectionate, but, when I saw his face redden and his eyes roll as I hit yet another screamer into a grove of pine trees, I couldn't help but believe that those particular words were born of my personal and irredeemable incompetence.

Fifteen strokes seemed like a pretty decent cushion as we mounted the tee box and surveyed the valley in front of us, the Katzenjammer foursome in front of us still zipping back and forth in their carts. On the previous tee it had been twenty, and I'd been comfortable enough with the way I played that hole to actually record the extra stroke I took to tap the ball in when my four-foot putt circled to the right just as it came within half an inch of dropping into the hole. In golf school they taught us that, as the day wears on, a ridge frequently builds up around the hole, like the crater of a volcano.

This ridge is from all the golfers who plant themselves a foot to six inches from the cup and then put all their weight on the green while they reach down to retrieve their ball, or who pull up some earth around where the cup is cut as they fish the ball out with their putters. This one-two effect can be pronounced, but now at least I know why putts slide around the target, although I don't always remember that in advance. But since I know the unfairness is visited on me in the midst of all the other unfairnesses that constitute this strange game, I sometimes allow myself to deduct the stroke, like when I'm rushed by other players or distracted by their conversation or their less than firm grip on the particularities of golf etiquette. But this hole was down the home stretch, when I wanted to be scrupulous, and I'd pushed the putt because I hurried it out of annoyance that the twelve-footer I had so carefully arced down the sloping green had missed the hole by about half an inch and slid six feet into Nowheresville.

The game we play is casual golf, friendly golf, the kind you play for fun, and you make jokes at yourself and your opponent while you're at it. Golf with a few mulligans and a little humor. We don't play Bill Clinton–level mulligans—very few do (and I say that as a lifelong Democrat)—but off the tee and occasionally when you hit a disastrous shot where it will take you eight days to find the ball, we just drop one and opt for a recount. Such a play is not by the "Rules of Golf," which are very strict, but close enough for government work, as we used to say, and as Clinton must often have said himself.

So I take another tee shot. That is allowed, especially since there is a housing project next to this hole and I once watched a kid steal all four drives from a foursome I was part of, by dashing onto the fairway, scooping up the balls with both hands, and tear-assing off into the woods. Any ball in those woods was ipso facto the property of the housing authority and its tenants. My second shot pops high into the sky on the other side of the fairway, settling near the green of the previous hole, but with the current green in view. It's a shortish hole anyway. I have room to work.

Earlier, when we came to the turn after the ninth hole, I found I had shot a 48, ten strokes better than usual, and my son was only two strokes behind because, at the age of nineteen, he has a body like a blacksnake whip and can crank the club around like an airplane propeller. Since it's not the length of the swing but the speed of the club head that makes the ball go whoosh and zoom, he outdrives me by about twenty or thirty yards on most holes, smiling as he observes the results. But half the time he putts like he's cross-eyed, so there's life in the contest yet. Today he was having trouble with his old reliable wedge, a weapon he can normally use to get the ball nicely up in the air for a soft landing and even (speaking of physics) to hit it crisply enough to get some backspin on it, which requires a matching of microscopic closeness between the grooves on the club and the dimples on the ball. I like to watch him hit these shots. I bought him a couple of lessons from a pro when we were on vacation about six years ago, and the rest he's figured out through trial and error and actual athletic ability, a generation-skipping trait in my family. I went to golf school a couple of years later, so I don't embarrass myself anymore and we can play together, now that he whips me at tennis unless he happens to be rusty from a long layoff.

I shoot under 120 and often under 110. But it's still double-bogey golf, two over par on every hole. Take 72 for par, add two strokes for each of the eighteen holes, and you come in at 108. Of course, you never just go two over on every hole. You par a few, you bogey a few, and you melt down and take the fabled snowman eight, or nine or ten, when your arms tighten up and you skull the ball off the toe of the club at a 75-degree angle to where you're aiming. Then the ball ricochets off a limb that looks too thin to stop anything as hard as a golf ball. But it kabooms right back at you, hits you in the knee, and rolls into the exposed root socket of an oak some sadistic course designer had the foresight to plant there half a century ago. Busting loose from there would take a chain saw, so you secretly lift the ball out and don't take the penalty stroke and feel bad for the rest of the round, or you take the stroke and hate yourself forever because of how it makes your score even worse than it was. Averages are deceiving. There is always a shot that brings you back, some eagle flight across water you didn't think you could cross or some roller-coaster thirty-five-foot putt that drops and you knew you had the line right all along. There are the meltdown holes, where the real score is 13 or 15, when you hack and foozle your way from tee to green in what seems like more time than it took Lewis and Clark to explore the entire Louisiana Territory.

As we approach the green, my son is having one of those holes. The trusty wedge, the one he sometimes slides into his belt like a rapier after dropping the ball to within three or four feet of the pin, is providing shots with lift but no thrust. He's short each time. This time he's in a little stand of rough. It's rained lately, and the mower hasn't been this way in a while. It's a public course, so they let the grass grow a little because of the constant beating it takes. Two weeks ago we had a six-hour round because there was a company picnic for beginners and the course managers were ferrying new cartons of balls to people on the back nine because they had already lost their original allotment of twelve.

My son hits three wedges and then three putts, the last putt to finish after he left the second one four inches short. With his drive, that gives him a seven. He holds up seven fingers, even more laconic than usual. Last fall at another public course, he hit his tee shot to the front of the green on a par three. I bounced on and over, and it took me a while to find my ball in the pile of leaves up against the chain-link fence that defined the back of the property. I holed out in four and asked him what he'd gotten. "Five," he said, nothing more. How could you take a five? I asked. You were on the front edge of the green in one. He turned toward the next tee, saying, as best as I could hear, "This is not a good time to talk to me." That was a sentiment I could identify with, sympathize with, relate to. My second shot hangs up on the edge of the green, I hit my wedge a little short and two putt, but it's still a five, my quota, and I'm on track.

I let him tee off first at the next hole. After one complete flub, which results in his asking me not to stand behind him where he can't see me, he hits a moon shot about 100 yards out, in the right rough, high grass with a fence in the way. I leave my tee shot short—it's a long par three—but I hit it straight onto the front apron of the green. Last week I birdied this hole with a twenty-five-foot putt that looped in like a Bert Blyleven curve ball. He finds his ball, plays it, and bangs it off the fence, but it bounces in the direction of the hole, under some trees on the right. The flag is about four feet back from the front of the green, so I don't want to over-hit my approach, a bump-and-run low-bouncing shot that I can usually get close to the hole.

But just like Tolstoy's brother challenging him not to think about white elephants, the thing I focus on, over-hitting, is exactly what I do, so I end up farther away on the green than I was on the fringe. My son hits a beautiful low-approach shot out of the woods and saves his five with a fifteen-foot putt that gets nothing but the bottom of the cup, a two-stroke improvement over the last hole, which I congratulate him on before I two putt from twenty-five feet. Three putt, actually—but he's not watching, and I got distracted with his problems and rooting for him to get it together, so the rule about how I give myself the short putts in certain situations seems applicable. Besides, I don't want to come into eighteen, which is a weird hole, under too much pressure, so I write down a four. If I had taken my time, I would have sunk the putt—it's the kind I almost never miss, short and straight, although I missed the same kind two holes ago. But it's getting a little late and I don't want to hold up our play, so I give myself the benefit. Rationalization is the key club on many occasions.

The last time I played number eighteen was right after my birdie, the second of my life. My first one came during a round of 136 and was almost a hole in one, but it was hard to enjoy fully because that was also the day I got a margin call from my stockbroker on my account, and my doctor called and said my cholesterol was over 275 and it was time I started cleaning up my act. My son had been with me that day, too, and we'd had fun—my fun watching him figure out one aspect or another of the game and get better, almost visibly, hole by hole at the age of sixteen, five foot ten and 110 pounds, and his fun discovering for the first time how far you can really send the ball when you're in the groove, not to mention how close you can come to the hole if things are working for you. Sometimes I think his hat must weigh more than he does, he's so skinny.

Last week, after my birdie here, I got stuck behind a three-some of giant female gym teachers who must have been specialists at some new sport they didn't have when I was in school. I was alone by then, my partners had called it a day, and while I waited, I checked the woods on both sides of the fairway and found eleven balls, most of them fairly new, many with the magic marker emblems that the dedicated public course golfer emblazons on his Top-Flite number 3 XL (for extra-long) 2000 or his Callaway 3 to distinguish it from the hundreds and hundreds of other balls that get whacked around any given course in a week's time. I also got poison ivy for the third time this year, so that part of my game definitely has to change because I itch all the time and it's put a serious crimp in other aspects of my adulthood.

I'm convinced those folks talk to the balls while they imprint their initials or three red dots or a green triangle, like the handlers at cockfights mutter confidently to their charges before strapping on their spurs and sending them into the ring to win or die. The bird understands nothing and the ball understands less, but human nature is what it is, and you use the tools you're given and do the best you can.

I play it safe this time, hitting a three wood that soars straight out far enough to reach the end of the bluff the tee box sits on and drop into the valley that leads to the final green. My son says nice shot and then launches one that looks like it probably has mine beaten by ten or twenty yards and asks me what I need to break a hundred.

Seven or better, I tell him, remind him of the eleven balls I found here last time I played when he was out of town, and head off into the woods, emerging five minutes later with eight shiny white spheres, most of them as good as new. There is no one anywhere behind us, so I'm not holding up play. He smiles approvingly and asks which club I want, mentioning that he just laid an eight iron up on the green and has a shot at par. Last time, after waiting for the gym teachers, I bounced my shot onto and over the green and into the pyracantha that divides the hole from the path back to the clubhouse. So I want a low shot that will just skip along and set me up for a nice little chip, two or even three putts and I'm in with a 97 or 98, new personal best, and how about that dad of yours, my boy. He'll be impressed.

But my first shot squirts right, more parallel to the hole than advancing toward it. When I take the club I initially thought to use but didn't, and relax and concentrate on just hitting a nice crisp clean shot, I smack the ball like King Kong, and I'm bouncing on and off the green again and into the selfsame thicket. Two wedges and one putt later, I'm four feet from the hole. If I drop it, I'm in at 99. He's already parred out with two putts from twenty feet, the second one an eight footer that rolled all the way around the rim before dropping, and he stands with his hands on his hips as I line up my attempt to make history. He's in the books with a 102, his best score ever and a strong finish.

When I was young, my father beat me at all the games we played. It was part of his making a man out of me. He showed me the tricks and the stratagems, along with things about odds in card games, by playing them on me. When we played counting card games and I failed to claim all my points, he would declare them as his, and a few of the games I lost were because of those, but more were because he was a better player, something I think was his real message to me. He never knew his father, who abandoned his mom before he was born, so he applied to me the lessons he'd learned in the U.S. Army, where he became a man himself. The fact that I was four, or seven, or twelve, when he beat me at one game or another didn't seem to factor into his set of needs and goals.

When my son was three, we were playing the card game Concentration on the sunroom rug at the place we had rented during the summer. In that game, after you lay out the whole deck facedown, if you turn over two cards that match, you get to go again, and whoever gets the most cards wins. When we came down to the end of the game, it was very close, and I turned over a five. There were only seven cards left, and we both knew where the other five was, but I picked a different card, which made it his turn, and he promptly scooped in the rest, smiling with glee and completely pleased with himself. My daughter had been watching the game from her perch on the back of one of the sofas.

"Dad," she said. "Dad."

"What?" I asked her. "What?"

"You never did that for me," she said.

I looked up at her and flashed an especially toothy smile. "Didn't I?" I said. "Didn't I?" She knew then, and a message I hadn't known how to convey got passed on, and I was so happy I almost cried. I was teaching them the most important lesson of all—how to be a winner—and my heart almost exploded with joy and relief.

I step up and hit the putt without letting myself think too much. In the hands of the gods. It skids right, just like on the last hole and two holes before that, and when I look up I see the wolfish glint of a smile on my son's mouth and in his eyes.

I'm better than him by two strokes, that's all. We're not a digit apart, my score in two digits and his in three. I may have won, but I didn't break 100 or come in with a new personal best. And he'll get me next time, I can see his body language saying, youth is waiting to be served, and soon. Sure, I say silently. We'll see, and inside myself on my heart sits a smile as broad as the orbit of Jupiter, the fullness of the circle resolved. I taught him how to win, and that is something he will always know, always.

XXXIX INNOCENTS ABROAD

DURING MY FOURTH YEAR as a lawyer, I finally bought my first suit that cost more than $200—a brown herringbone Canadian tweed with red and blue pinstripes alternating in the weave and a sort of pinched-in waist that would come to haunt me in the not too distant future. But when I bought it and started wearing the suit, it fit just fine. That was good, since my wife and I had planned a winter vacation. Our summer one had been canceled due to the illness of our senior partner, for whom I was doing a huge amount of work, so we had to wait for the work to be done and him to return before we could go anywhere.

This trip was to London and Paris, because in the wintertime there are many fewer tourists in both the Tourist Mecca and the Tourist Medina. It was a delayed honeymoon for us, also because of the senior partner's illness.

Because London is where Lloyds is headquartered, and because Lloyds was one of our firm's cornerstone clients, which meant a free lunch and a tour, I spoke to people who would know how to arrange things and got us a lunch date and tour. I didn't work on that account, or in the insurance area. But I was interested in how Lloyds functioned, and also to see how they comported themselves. Word in the firm was that they loved to encourage you to get the Dover sole, since the fish came whole and the Brits apparently loved to watch the uncultured and poorly brought-up Americans try to fillet the fish without mangling it.

I had already planned to order shrimp curry, because no one can fault you for that order, and I had started to relax as our host, Jeff, pointed my wife toward the ladies' room while we went one door farther over. At the exit to the men's room that is part of the Lloyds dining room stands a man of a certain age in a morning coat and striped trousers holding a whisk broom. His job in life is to remove as much dandruff as possible from the shoulders of the members and their guests. As we washed up and started for the door, Jeff asked me if I'd care for a dust-off. I said no, I thought I was all right, and I heard him say, sotto voce (which was odd, because only the two of us were there at the moment, unless you include the whisk-broom chap), "No, don't suppose you'd need one with that sort of a suit, would you now."

I can, in fact, still hear his voice as he said it. While I had laid my plans properly to avoid a Dover sole debacle, I had stumbled right into a brown suit blunder, which I now realized by waking up to the fact that every single man in the room was wearing a charcoal gray or navy blue suit. I almost wished I had brought my clown face, wig, and bubble-shaped red shoes to complete the effect, but it was too late now.

Throughout the lunch, I could hear everything that people were not saying much better than what they were saying. "How's the weather in New York this time of year?" became "Which part of Kansas did you say you came from?" and so on and so on. I have no recollection of any topic of conversation that we touched on throughout the entire forty-five-minute meal and was still cringing inwardly when we trooped back to Jeff's office for a ceremonial good-bye.

It hadn't taken me long to see that this was Jeff's job: greeting "dignitaries" or other "notables," seeing them back to where they had come from, and arranging tickets or whatever else visitors might need. I was anything but a dignitary or notable. Still, I was being hosted by, in essence, a concierge.

To my surprise, Jeff waved us into the seats across from his desk and grabbed the phone, punching in a string of numbers and then immediately speaking French in what seemed a pretty good imitation of the language. He spoke, he listened, he spoke, he listened, and finally he turned to me and said, "Okay. We're all set. Bernard de Canecaude, our representative in Paris—and France as a whole, for that matter—will pick you up tonight at your hotel and show you around a bit. You know, dinner, a cabaret, and the like. Then it turns out that tomorrow night he is having a party in Versailles, where he lives when he's not at his chateau in Normandy, and you are invited. Sensational fellow. I'm sure you will both have a fantastic time. Well, then, it's been a great pleasure to meet you, and I hope we see you again in the not too distant future." I was a clodhopper, all right, but apparently I was their kind of clodhopper, so no worries, mate, and on we went.

Bernard, as he insisted that we call him, was the genuine article. Debonair, well dressed, quick on the draw with drink orders, suggestions on the menu, and interesting topics to discuss, plus an unearthly speediness at getting up just before my wife did, so he could assist her from her chair and point her in the direction she wanted to go at that moment. He did it all so much in character, and with no self-consciousness, that we were put at ease in spite of ourselves, and felt as if we had become best friends despite having been with him only through drinks and dinner. Then he led us not far away to a place that had amazing Dixieland jazz, with all black musicians and clearly evolved from New Orleans, but thoroughly Frenchified, making it more complicated and unpredictable. Mesmerized, I lost myself in the intricacies of the instruments as they interwove, while Bernard took the opportunity to chat up Madame. In a way, the evening was the beginning of our vacation/honeymoon, and it was outstanding!

That night it snowed like crazy. But the following day we had the pleasure of visiting Versailles, covered in white, with perhaps twenty or thirty people in the whole place. We wandered for hours, throwing snowballs, walking around in the Petit and Grand Trianons with no one else around but a single guard who pretended he wasn't there, or we weren't. It felt, for lack of a better word, royal in the extreme.

We headed to Paris, a short train ride, to catch some winks and prepare ourselves for the dinner party we'd been invited to, then arrived back at the Versailles station, a few blocks from where we'd just been, a perfectly appropriate five minutes late. Madame de Canecaude was gorgeous, and their daughter of fifteen or seventeen was also perfect in every way. If there had been a magazine named *Elegance!* the family would have been on the cover at least twice a year, along with their dog, a black Lab named Truffe, which is French for *truffle*. I had worn my best and only suit. This is France, I told myself, not stuffy old England.

Aperitifs in hand, we looked over the art in the apartment. Delacroix pen-and-ink drawings, a small Corot, and a Degas pastel were among the items I spotted. Then a group of guests who had apparently arrived together burst in, and the party was on. Mrs. de C took charge of my wife and Bernard of me, and I met a number of insurance company directors and executives and a man who, from what I understood, was high up at Citroën. When he found out that I had lived in Richmond, Virginia, during college, he expostulated on the wonders of that city, which he had visited several times on business.

"What a wonderful life you lead there, in Richmond," the gentleman from Citroën exclaimed. "Almost *ancien régime*. You get up late, have breakfast almost at lunchtime, spend the afternoon riding with the hounds, finish with dinner and dancing at the Country Club of Virginia, and then go home to bed to be fresh for doing it again the next day. *Magnifique!*"

I agreed entirely. My family had moved there after I graduated from high school in Fairfax County, far north in oh so many ways from Richmond and all it spoke for. At Princeton, I knew about twenty guys from Richmond from classes and the dorms and my job as a busboy, but during the summer after my freshman year, I had no contact with any of them, possibly because none of them came home, Richmond being a candidate for a "dullest burg" award. I was laboring my way through Hugh Thomas's *The Spanish Civil War* and putting in eight hours a day; which shift depended on when they needed me to help cover vacation hours in the pack-and-ship department at Reynolds Metals in Bellwood, halfway between Richmond and Petersburg. My nickname there was College.

The first week, my fellow workers warned me twice to slow down and stop making them look bad. I had to promise the foreman to return to the Ivy League instead of spending the rest of my life making thirteen dollars an hour packing material for shipment to the customer, and hauling out the bent and busted stuff for credit and re-smelting. Thirteen dollars was real money back in the '60s, but I knew life must have something better in store for me than sitting around at three a.m. eating lunch outside on the night shift because it was still over 100 degrees in the enormous corrugated-aluminum shed. Every day I drank about six bottles of soda—lemon lime was my favorite—sixteen ounces each, and sweated it all off. By the time the summer was over, I had managed to lose all the beer and ice cream weight I had gained that freshman year. Almost.

My life in Richmond, obviously, had been somewhat different from the Country Club of VA. The Tuesdays and Wednesdays I had off didn't really allow for finding any women to get to know, so I mostly roosted poolside outside our apartment complex, reading and praying for an angel to emerge from the water (or at least the apartment building), but none ever did.

I shared none of this with Monsieur and instead held up my end of the conversation by telling him of our wonderful afternoon at the home of the Sun King in deep snow. As we were talking, and when another fellow came over to say hello and see who I was, I noticed that Truffe had stationed himself next to me. I could feel the curly top of his head nestle under my hand, and I petted him while conversing. A few minutes later, dinner was announced, and we went into what seemed like a large dining room for an apartment, until I realized that this apartment had two floors that went the length of the building.

Truffe sat down next to me and enjoyed whatever I was able

to slip him without anyone knowing I had found a secret love. I have loved dogs all my life. Since we moved every year when I was growing up, they were my wonderful and reliable companions, devoted listeners when we just sat and watched a stream go by or did nothing with great calm. So I slipped Truffe little tidbits, rubbing his dome and feeling quite at ease, due to the wine and the company.

We adjourned to the drawing room for dessert and after-dinner drinks. A short time later, we heard music, and Madame de C crossed the floor, took my hand, and led me back into the dining room, which had now become a discotheque, complete with disco ball. As we walked in, I understood why she had invited me to dance. I had wanted to bring the Canecaudes a special gift, and a bottle of wine was like coals to Newcastle. So I had brought them the latest two Rolling Stones albums, one of which was playing "Satisfaction" now. Madame de C and I fell into some sort of rhythm, but I really don't recall how my feet moved. We danced the whole record through, as others quickly filled the floor, spinning and whirling.

During a breather, I managed to say, while catching my breath, "This is wonderful. Thank you so much. What a fabulous party!"

She smiled and said, "No, thank you!! Our daughter will love it and think we are much cooler than we actually are, not to mention that the music is *fantastique*."

Truffe sauntered over and again sat next to me, ready for head-patting. I noted, "I also see I have a friend for life. He follows me everywhere. I do love dogs, and it's wonderful to connect like this. In Manhattan, it's not fair to keep a dog while both of us have full-time jobs, so this is a rare treat. I hope Truffe feels the same way."

"Oh, I'm sure he does," Madame de C said. "Although I believe he thinks he's about to go out shooting, and fetching the birds you kill while wearing your fashionable brown hunting suit. But he will get over it, and life, in its way, will go beautifully on."

XL ON DEMAND

SAY YOU ARE WORKING on a *New York Times* Saturday cross-word, separated but not divorced, and your beloved Dachsie, Lady Gwendolyn, whose custody you have agreed to share, is snuggling next to you in your black leather Brazilian armchair, she being the best thing you managed to pull out of the disaster of your marriage, even if it was only half of her. Plus, say it's almost noon, and you need to reduce said puzzle to smithereens before you finish your morning Bloody Mary and head out to whatever might be awaiting, smart but relaxed gent that you are.

While you are keenly focusing on 22 across, the message HOSTILE FRAGILE SENILE arises in your mind, without any sense that you have to write it down anywhere. Finally, suppose you recognize the phrase as the motto of your best friend Tony's over-fifty rugby club, down in D.C. You register that fact and go forward into a day and a date night—not fantastic, but good, and of some promise.

Then, on Monday morning, your phone rings while you are ironing your trousers and you pick it up and his very voice sounds out and asks, "*Amigo mío*, do you have any of our rugby shirts?" You promptly say no, but thanks for thinking of me, not exactly knowing why.

And he says, "You're a 2XX, right?" You acknowledge that being the truth, and he tells you that after the game Saturday he had gone to their clubhouse, found they were having a sale, and bought you one, which you should receive soon.

Then you ask him what time last Saturday this occurred, and he tells you very close to noon. "Outstanding, compadre," you say. "And let's say that the time I'm hearing what you did was almost exactly the time that the words on your club emblem ran through my mind. AWESOME. Beautiful."

"Really? Wow. Outstanding."

"I would agree," I said. "How cool is that?" We finish off the conversation by agreeing that the incident merited further exploration in our regular session next time we met. He had helped engineer me into a board chairmanship, which had earned me a nice chunk of change over more than twenty years. Most of that time I had served as a director, but then the founder retired, and people ID'd me as the obvious candidate for chairman, largely because there wasn't much extra money in it, and they all had real jobs.

Additionally, I had been on the board long enough to size up our advisors. Over time, you grew to recognize those who had a good understanding of their jobs, those who were essentially clueless, and our outlier, who was always within 10 percent of the S&P and kept liquid. But whenever we asked him for a deeper understanding of his strategy, he would start quoting Warren Buffett (his fund was based in the upper Midwest) and, if you tried to get past that double shuffle, would refer you to the financial statements and notes. We finally decided not to dig more deeply but to keep watching the numbers. By the way, the clueless ones didn't last long. What I'm really trying to say is that knowing the sheep from the goats helped me get a very reasonable return on my IRA.

Aside from that, Tony was my closest friend due to his wit and energy. At just short of seventy, he had been tackled in Aspen during a rugby game and stretchered off the field. The surgeon said afterward that the total separation of his patella tendon had simply finished a job that the condition of the kneecap indicated had mostly occurred years before. "Oh my god," Tony exclaimed, "that must have been the night during law school at NYU when I was chasing these two Village bozos down Bleecker and a fire hydrant jumped out in front of me and brought me low."

Several weeks after our conversation, I was at a pub in Morristown, New Jersey, where I lunched about once a week. This time I ended up discussing genealogy with a younger fellow I hadn't met before. Since I neither know nor care about that subject, I thought hard about how to change it. So I asked him if he believed in ESP.

"I honestly don't know," he said. "Do you?"

"Absolutely and positively. You want to hear why?" We ordered another beer, and I told him how Tony and I had managed to connect, across about five hundred miles, apropos of the Poltroons' rugby shirt, which has a broad yellow stripe down the back, since Poltroons means cowards in English military inside talk. The shirt itself is sensational—blue, yellow, and green, with a crest embroidered on it bearing the words you read earlier in capital letters. I wear it with great pride and relate rugby stories Tony has told me that I sometimes pass off as my own.

"Wow. Cool," my new friend said. "Could you do that for me?"

"Well," I responded, "why I believe it works is that the people involved are connected, as he and I are, because of a lot of years we've spent in each other's company doing stuff together. Also, neither he nor I knew that it would occur." At that moment I realized I needed to shift the conversation to a different topic.

"Let me tell you a little bit about why he's my best friend," I said. "He signed up for the Marines Platoon Leaders Corps program, which required you to go through basic training, and then after college, you became a second lieutenant. They announced a contest among the three companies in the program at the time. Each side had five contestants, who competed in a race that involved four different paths that interconnected in various ways so that each group of contestants saw the others going past. The prize was a week off KP. Those who didn't win would share KP duty. To determine the winner, you would just add up the times of each set of contestants.

"At Quantico, where Tony trained, it was well over a hundred degrees when the squads went out for that event. He was second or third after the first of five trips around the format, with two guys on his team close and two guys nowhere. As they continued to run, he figured out that he had a pretty good spot and felt that if, on each round, he grabbed the rifle, helmet, or field pack of one of the slowest on his team, they would pick up more speed than he would lose, and indeed his team won due to that strategy. I wish I'd been there to see him chugging along with three helmets, four rifles, and three field packs, but somehow he sussed out the winning strategy. Now, is that not unbelievably generous and incredibly strong? He told me he was five pounds lighter at the end of the hike."

"Yeah," my new buddy remarked. "But what about the ESP? I thought you were going to do one for me!"

"Oh," I said, and took a sip of my beer. It seemed as if I had pulled a fish from deep in the water, past whom I might be able to blow a fastball—mixing metaphors totally—as the guy sat next to me wide-eyed and open-mouthed. "Okay. Pick a number between seven and nineteen."

"Okay," he told me. "I'm ready."

"Good," I responded. Pausing for a moment and another theatrical draft of beer, I then asked, "What is it?"

"Eleven," he said, and I quickly replied, "That's right!"

"Wow," he marveled. "Cool. Awesome. Wow!" Luckily, food arrived just in time to obviate further conversation.

XLI EVERYBODY DOES IT

BACK IN MY FINAL DATING DAYS, I met a woman at my gym, where both of us were waiting for the director to return to address some minor issue. I had recently moved to Westwood, New Jersey, two towns north of where I had lived previously with my future ex-wife, although we were out of business, except for the division becoming official and signed in my blood. Lenore was a dazzling ray of sunshine in comparison, and I asked her to join me for lunch, which she kindly accepted.

Her story was like, and unlike, mine. She had just thrown out a guy she'd been with for twelve years and hadn't had sex with (or with anyone else) for the last five, so she thought while she still had rubber left on her tires she should take herself out for a spin, which was why she'd joined the gym. I had recently turned fifty-five and she was almost sixty, but the tune-up seemed to have worked. I found her open, cheerful, free of pretense, and sexy, as well as much younger than her age.

We were lingering over our wine, so I asked her what she had planned for the rest of the afternoon that she couldn't get done tomorrow. When she replied, "Enjoying you banging my brains out?," I called for the check to demonstrate what a gentleman I am. Her town house in a small development across from a country-style (not country club) golf course had a nice deck in the back and a hot tub in her capacious bathroom. We toweled off after an interactive shower and jumped on the bed after turning down the neatly tucked-in coverlet. That was when I realized that when a woman that age has sex after five years of inaction, you really have to take it very, very slowly, which I somehow managed to do, with results that were well worth the effort. Afterward, as they say in all the bodice rippers, neither of us was in any rush to go anywhere or do anything, so we didn't.

We had plenty to learn about each other and enough time to do so. I got to learn about Herbie, who had occupied her life until she realized he had been gone for years and she hadn't noticed, so she quickly made their break official. "He was a good bridge player, and he had a sense of humor and always pulled the chair out for me when we ate in a restaurant. But I think that's about it." We progressed on to her older brother, who had muscular dystrophy and lived in a nursing home, which she visited once a week, and a son, Jerry, who had married his Romanian secretary, whom he had hired through her mother, his cleaning lady. Jerry had switched from debt collection to helping people renegotiate loans they were in default on. He knew, having been on the other side, what creditors would accept as haircuts to keep out of bankruptcy and foreclosure, and he liked that side better. So after that he did well by doing good.

She looked across the bed as I was noodling her nipple with my thumb and finger and said, "Of course, there are also cheaters around who sign up and then start to Mickey Mouse you instead of doing what they said they would. Jerry has a guy named Ivan he turns those cases over to. You don't want to meet Ivan, I assure you. Put your mouth there and let's see what happens."

The best part was that we got along great with little back-and-forth, since we had seized an opportunity and made the most of it. I stayed the night, we watched *Shampoo* with Warren Beatty and Carrie Fisher, a movie I hadn't seen in years but could watch twenty times in a row and not be unhappy, and when I left I said I'd call, and I did. We discovered we had this "off the books" arrangement that allowed us to see each other and still do whatever else came up in our "real lives." I had no idea how long our setup would work, but why fight it? A part-time clinical psychologist who worked with several nursing homes and assisted-living places, she was very easy to get along with, her schedule was flexible, and I still remembered how to grill and mix drinks, so we made a good and useful team.

In addition, when Jerry and his family were on vacation (I think in New England, taking the kids to camp) we went over to his house and swam in the pool—in fact, got things going in the pool, a first for me. Also, she knew that the combination on the door of the office where Jerry hid his pot was his wife's birthday, backwards, so that also worked out well.

Her office had previously been out near Brighton Beach in Brooklyn, and her degrees were from Brooklyn College. Her first husband had been her professor and advisor, but ultimately she realized he was treating her like a lab assistant and a person to have children by, without much involvement. Teaching provided him with the perpetual opportunity to find fresh subjects for amusement among his newer students, so she canned him, after some serious research and shadowing by private detectives.

Her second husband, the love of her life, was named Rick. Since her first husband was Eric, it was hard to tell which one she was talking about until I got to know them from her descriptions.

After about ten wonderful years, Rick had died of a series of heart attacks, which gave rise to Herbie and now me. I loved her matter-of-factness, as when she said, "You know, Rick and I had a wonderful love life, and you're bringing it all back. I guess that was the problem with Herb: he reminded me too much of what I'd lost in Rick. Like you remember what's missing when you see a blank piece of paper instead of a man with a hard dick." She claimed Herb was probably the drone they worked from to create the robots they use now to kill people from a distance. "Here, just lie back and let Momma take care of the Deathless Dragon," she added, with what might have been a wink, or a nod.

Nothing wonderful ever remains private. Before long—Labor Day weekend, in fact—Lenore asked if I could escort her to a party her old friend, who happened to be her chiropractor with an office now in the Empire State Building, was throwing on Saturday "down the shore." So I called the friend who had invited me to a shindig where I thought I might get lucky, and asked for a raincheck. He said, "No prob," and our game was on.

. We took her car, but I drove. After some back-and-forth in Middleboro, in Middlesex Township, we found an extremely new development where no tree in sight was bigger around than my two big toes if you tied them together, and a substantial number of bicycles, balls, and other paraphernalia were strewn across sidewalks and newly sodded lawns—the epitome of a bedroom community.

This was where her dear friend Ivan lived, with his wife, Raisa, who had been Lenore's secretary in Brighton Beach when Ivan had set up his first practice across the hall. Ivan's driveway was full of cars, so we parked in the cul de sac and walked over with our swim gear and other stuff, including two bottles of wine. As happened in those days, the vague but unmistakable aroma of marijuana greeted us long before we found the party, which was in the back. A pool half-covered by a tent had a few chaises organized at one end and a bunch of kids bouncing around and splashing each other at the other. About thirty people were mingling, and music was playing, so it seemed we had picked a good time to arrive.

I met our hosts, the short and energetic Ivan and the taller, svelte, and languid Raisa. We got drinks and food and chatted for a bit, and Ivan led us over to a couple of chaises next to his parents, then buzzed off to see what needed addressing, shouting at the guy behind the barbecue, "We've got hungry people here, Dmitri. Let's get it in gear!"

Ivan's parents could not have been more delightful. He was a dentist, and she had been a concert pianist in Moscow. Now they lived in Brooklyn, and she gave occasional performances for charities and older people in assisted living. Every Wednesday, instead of playing golf like the other 200,000 dentists in Brooklyn and Queens, they had lunch near Lincoln Center and saw a matinee at the Metropolitan Opera. They were intelligent, pleasant, and easy to talk to, I thought, as I munched my way through the ribs, corn, and cole slaw.

"Well, you certainly taught your son how to throw a great party," I remarked when my mouth wasn't full. "I get the feeling he's the major domo and she's the queen." Lenore slapped me on the wrist with a grin, and we chuckled almost in unison. In the background, the word "Doctor" was being repeated over and over with unusual enthusiasm. "But what's with this 'Doctor' stuff I keep hearing? Do you know?"

They both laughed. "That's Ivan and his partners," his dad explained. "I can see three of them. Ivan's standing next to two, and the fourth one is over there with his kids in the pool. Ivan likes to say it to emphasize his professionalism and collegiality. It seems like every time they get together to discuss something, they have to refer to each other as Doctor, so they don't forget to act like one. Or something, I don't know. After about half an hour, you won't even hear it."

I went back to get a supplementary burger and found Ivan again berating the guy behind the grill with what struck me as a slightly overboard level of zeal. I turned so that the guy couldn't hear me and asked Ivan what was up with his grill-meister.

"If he *were* a grill-meister," he groused, vaguely gesturing over his shoulder in the fellow's direction, "that would be one thing, but he's essentially a lazybones who keeps forgetting to put his baseball cap on when he's cooking, and that's just the start. Here," he said, topping off my glass of wine, "come on over here and I'll spell it out for you." We took a few steps, and a man came by and shook Ivan's hand, each of them saying "Doctor," and we grabbed seats at the picnic table.

"Okay," he said. "You haven't met Raisa's parents yet, right? They're over there drinking and sunbathing. See them? So, he's their son, which is to say he's my brother-in-law. They had a plan for him to be a lawyer, and he had just enrolled in some law school in Brooklyn, so it seemed like things were in good shape, right? Then, as it turns out, his dad and mom were conspiring—their scheme was part of the reason NYC parking meters got switched over—with a guy who had the master key to all the parking meters in Brooklyn. Which is a big number, right? And they got said brother-in-law here involved because their English needed support to make the conspiracy happen. The parking-meter guy was from their old section of Moscow, and as soon as they met, they were on their way to Felony City.

"Guess what? When they got the key, they completely emptied every frigging meter they came to. They had so much change they only covered a couple of blocks, so they packed it in. The next time—systematic as the thimble-headed little people they proved to be—they went directly to the meter after the one where they had stopped siphoning the last time! And guess what? People noticed those facts, waited several nights at the meter they left off at the second time, and, as one might expect, they all ended up in jail. Did not pass 'Go' or anything like that. Everyone gets a year's vacation in downtown Brooklyn near the courts, and my beloved bro there finds himself ineligible for the world of law—except in the defendant's or parolee's seat, that is.

"Finally, Raisa makes me promise to take him into my practice. Doctor, hi there. So in the meantime I'm getting my money's worth out of him although he's much more lapse-arian than I had even imagined. But at least I'm getting laid again. Isn't she beautiful, my wife with the baggage? But a sweetheart and hot as hell. What can I tell you? Anyway, now you're in the know, and any friend of Lenore's is a friend of mine. Raisa was working with Lenore when I met her, and the rest is history, or our story. Anyway, I have to go crack the whip and call some more people Doctor, so I'll see you in a bit and you can tell me a story to match that one. Enjoy. Don't think too hard." He patted me kindly on the back and zoomed off as if he were riding a moped, or had three legs instead of two.

I wandered in the direction Ivan had pointed me to get a good look at Mom and Dad, both of whom were stretched out with a cigarette in one hand and a drink in the other. He sported a cut-off T-shirt, several million tattoos on his upper and lower body, and a pair of New York State–issue gym shorts, with some dollar flip-flops on the ground next to him. She was wearing a bathing suit that strained to encompass all she had to offer as if it might be marketable, although it wasn't. Over her eyes she wore eye protectors with holes in each eye cup so she could see enough to find her drink and smokes. I didn't stop for a second look.

On my way back to the center of the festivities, a guy asked me if I had a light, which I happened to, and then offered me a toke on his joint, which I cheerfully accepted. He was a doctor of podiatry, which I learned was a specialty also short of MD status, and the joint proved good enough that we smoked it cheerfully and spoke only of the weed itself. We nodded to each other in a vaguely official manner, said "Doctor," and I went to find Lenore.

She and Raisa were sitting by the sliding-glass doors to the kitchen. "Hi, sweetie," Lenore said. "We were just talking about how Raisa got her degree. I did all her papers, and they only had take-home tests, so I did those for her as well. She graduated with honors. How about that?"

"That's super," I said. "Good thing you got her married off in the bargain, so she never had to find an actual job that required knowing anything about what you learned for her or knew already."

"Oh, come on," Raisa laughed. "Everybody does it, right? Am I right or am I right? Lenore?"

"Of course you are, darling," she said. "Everybody."

XLII   FULL FORCE

RIDING IN OUR FRIEND'S CUSTOMIZED JEEP into Crown Heights, we felt we had the right vehicle for the trip. Many will remember that Crown Heights was the scene of the 1991 race riot that drove Mayor David Dinkins from office. The motorcade of Rabbi Menachem Schneerson, the leader of the Lubavitcher sect of Orthodox Judaism, had accidentally run over two children of Guyanese immigrants, killing one. This tragedy led to an eruption of anger from young black men, culminating in a gang of twenty or more assaulting and killing Yankel Rosenbaum, a Jewish student from Melbourne doing research for an academic thesis. Civic leaders joined forces to create a more peaceful atmosphere in this heavily crowded portion of the heart of Brooklyn, but Dinkins fell because of a general sense of inadequate police response to the riot.

Now, more than ten years later, it was easy to see how the unfortunate events could have come about. On one side of the street, on a lawn set beside several identical buildings that resembled Housing Agency apartments, a number of *shul* boys, wearing yarmulkes, white shirts, and black vests and trousers, played ball. Directly across, an almost equal number of black and Hispanic kids—sporting jeans belted below their creases and do rags, bandanas, or Mets and Yankees baseball caps, in all the colors of the rainbow—stood leaning against the storefronts of bodegas, cigarette shops, small markets, and the usual array of New York City neighborhood businesses, including hair and nail salons and two barbershops.

We were convoying to a meeting arranged by our friend, a white lawyer with a black wife who specialized in representing black music groups and anyone else in music who would pay for his services. Behind us was another car with several lawyers from our firm, a large, diversified business law firm that had recently acquired a small group also devoted to the world of music, film, and other lucrative arts. I was the finance guy, a specialist in secured lending and what had become known as "securitizations." We all know, too well, about CMOs, GMOS, CDOs, and the like, and our specialty was a subspecies of them. In our case, though, only one of our deals didn't pay out in full, as opposed to the tsunami of defaulted debt that nearly laid low the entire global economy and set off the Great Recession. This event occurred several years before the disaster that loomed ahead, so as we say when all else fails: "Who knew?"

The original version of these financings gave them the name "Bowie Bonds," due to David Bowie's first having used such a device to insulate himself and his estate from the draconian taxes levied on substantial estates in the U.K. The device is as simple as could be. Some assets that produce cash are identified—like royalties from a collection of oil wells, records, or songs—and put into a trust.

The transfer into the trust makes it a sale for legal purposes, but not for tax purposes, and capable of having a lien put on it to secure the debt the trust incurs. The owner gets the money from the debt offering, and the revenues from the asset supply the wherewithal to pay off the debt. At the end of the term, the property reverts to the original owner, but if you can make the term long enough (as happened with Bowie), the property stays outside the estate, and the heirs, not under the will but by terms of the trust, get the asset and future proceeds. But more on that later. Back to our drive.

Our meeting was with a rap/R&B group named Full Force, who had a well-established reputation in the NYC area. The six brothers and cousins sang, played different instruments, and performed, but more importantly they had produced a significant number of songs for Destiny's Child, 'N Sync, Boyz II Men, and other similar groups and artists. They were at the heart of hip-hop before it knew what it was and could be. The meeting was at their studio, and in a few minutes we arrived there. It was a brownstone of no distinction, in an area filled with more of the same, street after street. We entered through the kitchen and met our guys and their accountant, a white Jewish man who smiled but had little, if anything, to say.

The studio itself was in the basement of the building that housed the mother of three members of the group and had housed them until they got famous and slightly well off. That was part of the reason we were there. Like most groups, these guys had made a splash and then taken several years to get their business going. But they were signed right out of the box by a record company, which advanced them substantial amounts of cash to make them happy, feel like men of means, and adopt lifestyles and habits that might not have been the wisest but were typical of young men in their early twenties.

These advances bore interest at 22 percent, compounded daily, with the interest added to the principal up front. Life insurance companies do the same thing on all policy loans (and you know they were in on how that law got shaped), so the APR was actually meaningfully higher than the "face" amount of the interest on the loan, but somehow short of illegal. If anyone has any doubt about whether New York favors debtors or creditors, look at Wall Street, but shade your eyes so you're not blinded by the glow of greed and economic power. This was just an updated version of Tennessee Ernie Ford's song "Sixteen Tons," in which he dies owing his soul to the company store—or record company, as the case may be.

So we headed for the basement, ducking our heads on the way, and searched for seats in the twenty-foot-square room filled with instruments and recording and performing devices such

as amps, a console, and music stands. I recall sitting on a size-
able amp because next to it was a stand I could put my briefcase
on. I was in charge of handing out our presentations and giving
the spiel.

I ran through our routine. We had done a number of these
pitches, most prominently to Iron Maiden ("Bring Your Daughter to the Slaughter"), none of whose songs I have ever heard. I
had the privilege of going to London to finalize that deal, which
included buying lunch for their manager in a Marco White four-
star restaurant. He had been the president of his Oxford debating society and wore (to no one's surprise) a dark gray suit,
a striped blue and white shirt with white collar and cuffs, diamond cuff links, and an Oxford tie. He was personable, lovely
to lunch with, stories and all, and didn't quibble over my picking
up the check, which was not inconsiderable.

The Full Force crew scattered themselves among the available spaces, based on the principle of get what you can before
someone else does. There were two key elements. First, the numbers had to make sense, but that science and statistical hoo-ji-
bob had been well worked out before we came on the scene. (See
The Long Short for more explication of that science, especially the
part with the blonde drinking champagne in the bath, wearing
nothing but bubbles.) Second, the debt had to be non-recourse,
just like your mortgage: if you fail to pay, they can take your
house, but not your ass or your children. But it also means you
may lose the property, since that's the security for the loan.

At this point, I made sure to note that the Rolling Stones
were not on anyone's list to securitize. Not only did they own
their songs and make gazillions of dollars, so they didn't need
the up-front money securitization could provide, but also they
had faith in their long-term potential—coupled with the idea
that losing the songs was inconceivable to them, so why put the
songs at risk?

Liveliness ensued, due to the fact that these guys were also very bright, especially after having signed their birthright away for a mess of pottage at 22 percent vigorish. Plus, there proved to be a connection between finance and music that was first identified by Professor Howard Gardner of Harvard in his masterpiece, *Frames of Mind*, which reclassified intelligence into eight categories instead of simply mathematical and verbal. So, before you forget to write this down, music and finance follow extremely similar sets of rules, with wonderfully parallel escape routes into the byways and Immelmann turns available to anyone who speaks either language, and jump shifts can be beyond imagination. Gardner did his research on patients with various brain injuries from diseases and accidents, and Boston is the home of both, in more ways than one.

The kettle was starting to percolate, on the verge of overheating, when our senior entertainment partner threw up his hands and said, "Well, that's it in essence, guys, and we would love to figure out how we can do a deal with you. Bottom line."

Paul, the bass player, a six-foot-eight slender guy, proved to be the one everyone else in the group looked to at that moment. He was leaning on and filling the doorway from upstairs, and he squeezed his nose and looked at me. "I just want to ask you one thing, man. Honest to honest, man to man. If the songs don't sell, and the money don't show, what happens then?"

I smiled, which was weird, because up until then I had never done a deal that didn't work. Wall Street is littered with them, day in and day out, but not on my block. In thirty-five years, the only deal I ever worked on that didn't pay out was the Bill Blass deal, which was beyond weird in other ways, and not just because the CFO (one of the guys who was using the securitization to get the money to buy the business from Blass) had started as an outside auditor whose office was between Blass's and the changing room for the models, so he got endless eyefuls while working on the annual report and was not prepared to let that go for anything in the world.

"You're on the money, Paul," I said. "If the songs don't sell, they get the songs, because they didn't get the money. Foreclosure, pure and simple. Correct."

Paul stood up straight and put one hand in the air, forefinger extended, and said, "If the songs don't sell shit, the songs ain't worth shit. They can keep the mother-fucking non-selling songs. Non-recourse is going to be our new middle name." The beauty of this deal, as he went on to share with his brethren, was that it would enable them to get the 22 percent carry off their backs and make money for real, which would include setting up their own record company and helping save others like themselves from getting stuck and stung the same way, enslaved to the money people, never to escape.

It was like watching maple syrup being poured on fried chicken and waffles. Each in his own way, everyone in the room went "Oom, oom," without opening their mouths, but all of us could hear the sound, which also sounds more than a little like "Ka-ching!" Michael, our senior guy, said, "Okay, then. Let's set up a schedule, get together at our office next week, and go for the gold." Michael could sell, too, and it was sweet to see him deliver the two in our one-two punch. A knockout, no ifs, ands, or buts.

We shook hands, even with the accountant. Then we packed up our stuff, kissed Mom in the kitchen on our way out, did a few high-fives to accentuate what a good meeting it had been, and started counting the money in more or less the same way our prospective clients had started doing downstairs.

Happily, that was a good day's work. We still had a lot to do—verify the copyrights, confirm the receipts and over what time they had come in (longevity is highly important in this area, for rating agencies and investors alike). So on the sidewalk in front of Mom's we shook hands, agreed to meet first thing the next morning to start turning wax into gold, and went home with a very sweet bedtime story for our nearest and dearest.

Which made it all the harder to learn the next day that the reason the accountant had so little to say was that he was working as hard as he could to avoid telling the guys that his firm's warehouse had burned to the ground two days before, and that among the ashes on the site lay all the basic financial information that would be needed to validate the rating we would need to sell the mother-fucking bonds.

That close! Reconstructing the info could take as long as three or four years. We were that close, for them and for us, but *No* was the name on the door and, in that case, always would be. We did other deals, like for the guy who wrote "Money (That's What I Want)" and "I Heard It Through the Grapevine," and one involving James Brown, where he signed his name everywhere with an X, but this deal could have been so cool, so right, so good, except for fate and all that can signify.

XLIII SHABAT SHALOM

AT THE HEIGHT (or nadir) of the period of huge dollars being poured into the construction of nuclear power plants in the 1980s and '90s, I had the good luck (professionally) to be at one of the leading law firms in America involved with the electrical utility industry. My role involved helping four or five companies issue billions of dollars of securities at a breathtaking pace. Two of them, Central Maine Power and LILCO, canceled their plants, but Portland General (later, part of Enron, to their misfortune) and Niagara Mohawk each put the hammer down and sold tons of bonds, preferred stock, and common stock over a number of years. I created a terrific team of lawyers that made these deals relatively economical. They did all the mechanical elements and I wrote the disclosure, because I was closest to the facts. I was also the only one who could strike enough fear into the execs to get them to tell more of the truth than they ever wanted to—like the continuing fact that there really was no reliable budget or expected completion date for any of the units.

In one case, a private report was issued for one client by INPO (Institute of Nuclear Power Operations), a group of U.S. Navy Rickover veterans who had been through the nuclear submarine corps, and who had clear understandings of full disclosure and unwarranted optimism. I was told that the report was confidential and could not be shown to anyone outside the management group. Then I discovered that all the INPO reports to other nuclear companies were included in the documents filed with the Securities and Exchange Commission in connection with annual filings, and I sent the list of those reports to the board. So I finally got my own copy. Several things seem worth remembering.

First, the existing reactor now in service had a control board that showed where the cesium rods were in terms of their depth in the uranium core, where they served to control the pace of the nuclear reaction. About 40 percent of these rods showed they were fully inserted at all times, which would give you relative comfort. But the correct reading would show up only when you tapped the glass enclosure of each dial, watched it spring alive, and then go to the correct reading, which was always different from the default version. The company had a five-year plan to replace the rods that didn't work, even though they were their first line of defense against disaster!

In one case, the INPO inspector happened upon five men standing around a port in the floor, inside of which a sixth man knelt, welding. He asked the foreman whether the man was qualified to perform that weld and got the clear answer "I got him in the hole, don't I?" This plant had a lively black market in clean urine for passing drug tests. If you saw all the gun racks in the pickup trucks in the parking lot and the Allman Brothers T-shirts, it made perfect sense. The inspector went to the records department and found the man's name missing from the list of welders qualified for that kind of work. But later he learned that was because the records department was three years behind in updating the list.

Which leads indirectly to the fact that during one year we did so many deals involving first mortgage bonds that one issue was dated August 28, so we could get it closed and on the books before the end of the month, to show the company's strong cash position involving unspent future nuclear investments. Historically, all utility mortgage bonds paid on the first or fifteenth of the month (fifteenth only in thirty-day months—no bonds in February) because that simplifies all the calculations.

Our system was highly routinized. We had about fifty documents that were required under the 1927 First Mortgage Indenture and Deed of Trust with Marine Midland Bank, Trustee, that governed the bonds—their issue, payment, redemption, and so on. None of these documents required my looking at them, and the trustee's lawyer reviewed all of them, so the company's representative had only to glance at them and sign them once the lawyer gave the thumbs-up. We always hosted the closings. My role was to show up from time to time and check in with my team. Then I would sit and talk with Rich, the trustee, for an appropriate amount of time even though essentially we had nothing to say to each other, but we were the only people in the room with nothing really to do. I would sign the opinions at a certain point, but his signing the cross-receipts our client's CFO had signed days before was the climactic event, and that would be tomorrow. Then I would buzz out and come back in an hour or two, do basically the same drill, and show up the next morning at the closing to confirm the recording of the supplemental indentures in thirty-five upstate counties, and the movement of the funds from the underwriters to the trustee to the company. Then we were ready for another deal in two or three weeks.

The timing of the bond issue opened a new avenue of conversation for Rich and me, when he asked what I was doing for the holidays. I was quasi-Jewish enough (curly-haired, graying, glasses, and smart ass) to know he didn't mean Christmas or Labor Day, but I'm also enough of a wise guy not to miss an opening like that for a good leg-pull. The fact that I didn't realize how good it was didn't emerge until much, much later. (The head of the Israeli crew team returns from a trip to Hahvahd University to see if they can improve their performance and stop losing all the time. He bursts into the coach's office and shouts, "Coach— I've got it. Over there, they have eight guys rowing and only one guy yelling!") I have a large number of wonderful Jewish friends of many years, at least until this story gets out. ("Help!

My son the nuclear physicist who calls me every Friday night is drowning!")

So I took the opportunity to share with him the fact that, after services for Rosh Hoshana, we were having our rabbi and his family over for a meal and some readings. He responded quickly by telling me that he belonged to a very progressive congregation in Westchester, and they were including a Navajo chief in their ceremonies for both Rosh Hoshana and Yom Kippur. Duly impressed, I said I'd pass that on to the head of our temple and maybe get back to him about how we might also manage that.

If you know your Jewish calendar, you will see where we're going. If you don't know it, get a calendar from the famous Hasidic camera shop—once 47th Street Photo, now B&H—behind the main post office and a block from Penn Station, just to look at all the days they are closed, which will fill you in efficiently. Years ago I bought a camera at that same store, paying in cash. I received a 1943 zinc penny as part of my change, and, having been born that year, I said, "A very good year, 1943." The woman at the cash register replied, "Not such a good year, really," with a theatrical but genuine sigh, and I looked up to see everyone else behind the counters in the small store nodding, and in some cases tugging at their payos (men's sidelocks, long enough to tug at, manifesting distress).

Autumn is littered, like fallen leaves, with Jewish holidays: Succoth, Simchas Torah, several others I can't remember because I'm not really Jewish. This meant I saw Rich a number of times during the fall, and for each occasion I had to come up with another story. To conform to my approach, the stories had to be both traditional and new in some way consistent with each other and our sense of togetherness. One time I even used the word *mittenbrot* as we stood next to each other selecting sandwiches for lunch. He looked at me quizzically, and I chuckled and said it was a joke, so then we both chuckled together.

But all good things must come to an end, and hopefully all

bad things as well, because the deeper I got in this hole I had created for myself, the guiltier I felt, becoming as it were more Jewish by the day, which, necessarily, involved a lot of discomfort, uncertainty, and *tsuris*, if you get me.

Jack, my client's CFO, called right after Thanksgiving to announce that he believed it was time to have lunch with our trustee, Rich, to discuss the relationship between them and the company. Time stopped for a moment as I considered what this really meant. The relationship was spelled out in the Mortgage Indenture, all 348 pages written in stone in 1927, brought down from the Mount Sinai of capitalism and secured debt, and amended only twice, by enormous effort and compelling necessity. So, I thought, what's to discuss?

Time continued to stop, as Death did for Emily Dickinson, and then I got it. The CFO had a serious girlfriend in the company, and what better treat for the woman in your life who is not your wife than a trip to New York City for the holidays. The first week in December is also the time that financial execs from all the major utilities, nationwide, come to the city for a feeding frenzy held by the major underwriters who do almost all their deals, in various rotations and combinations. Jack was not a joiner, so he undoubtedly planned to mix a considerable amount of pleasure with what was necessary on the business side, accept whatever hospitality was offered by the bankers, and charge his own costs to the company.

"Yeah, Jack," I said. "Sounds good. All the Utility Finance Week social stuff is in the evening, so let me check with Rich and we'll find a good day to do lunch." (Lunch was "done" in those days, as opposed to now, when you get the soup packet from the kitchen, pour boiling water into your little reinforced paper bowl, salt and pepper to taste, and take it back to enjoy at your desk.) I called Rich. We set a date. The next thing you know we were sitting in Charlie O's, the famous steakhouse one door away from 30 Rock, and all that connotes vis-à-vis the

Christmas Tree, NBC, GE, Exxon Mobil, and Saks across the street, near where Atlas holds up the globe that carries us all, for all to see, at the Crossroads of the World.

The girlfriend was, of course, not on the roster for lunch. More likely she was at Saks, where Jack would meet her later and produce the resources to buy her something nice to wear at dinner. It will not escape the close reader that I had gone from simply lying to conspiring to defraud in a very short time. I had always been a real Boy Scout when it came to ethics and proprieties involving everything but golf balls at Christmas. Now, I was the front man for the whole *meshugas* (calamity of confusion), and using a "fellow Jew" as my mustache.

My breath was coming deeper and slower as I walked into Charlie's, considering how to pull myself out of this torture chamber of my own creation, although admittedly with some help from Jack. We chatted amicably and superficially for the time necessary to get two martinis down the hatch, and then Jack excused himself, saying that he needed to clear his thinking before deciding whether he wanted his steak rare or medium rare, and headed off for the men's room. This was the moment I had been waiting for. As the waiter brought our third martinis, the ones we would substitute for red wine with the steaks, Rich leaned over and asked me how my Chanukah had been. "It's been a while since I saw you. Did you have a big group over?"

I looked longingly at the third "see-through," as we called them, that the waiter had just provided me, but restrained myself. Not now, growled a voice even I could hear. I leaned over toward Rich and explained that I really had to apologize and felt bad for having misled him over the past few months. At first, the deception had struck me as funny, and now I understood just how wrong that judgment that had been. I apologized from the bottom of my heart, I said, "because the fact is, I'm not Jewish at all."

I could see Jack coming back up from the underground lavatory, and in that moment I looked down, because I felt Rich's hand on my forearm, just below where my cuff ended. Flesh on flesh.

In a half-whisper, accompanied by a smile of thoroughgoing solidarity, he said, "I understand," squeezed my arm for a half-second, and that was it. "Go for it! I've got your back!" was what he didn't say, but that's what he meant, so the deal was sealed. Not the one I wanted, but the one I had earned, in a way I could never report, except here. It's funny to consider that this story is a confession by a collapsed Catholic of leaving yet another faith, but somewhat "mensa mens," as they sort of say. I came back to the fact that my intentions had been good, and now the result was good. The fact that all in between had been considerably less than good was beside the point. And the steak, with the traditional steamed spinach accompaniment, was as good as I hadn't even dared hope for.

PRODUCED BY
WILSTED & TAYLOR
PUBLISHING SERVICES

Project manager Christine Taylor
Production assistant LeRoy Wilsted
Copy editor Melody Lacina
Designer and compositor Michael Starkman
Proofreader Nancy Evans
Printer's devil Lillian Marie Wilsted
Printer and binder Bookmobile